STAN
CULLIS

STAN CULLIS

The Iron Manager

A BIOGRAPHY BY JIM HOLDEN

breedon **books**
PUBLISHING

First published in Great Britain in 2000 by
The Breedon Books Publishing Company Limited
Breedon House, 3 The Parker Centre, Derby, DE21 4SZ.

Paperback edition 2005

ISBN 1 85983 492 2

Printed and bound by Biddles Ltd, King's Lyn, Norfolk PE30 4LS.

Contents

Dedication

For Henni and Bill

Acknowledgments

THIS book could not have been written without the marvellous co-operation of so many people. First and foremost, my thanks must go to everyone in the Cullis family, who supported the project from the outset and allowed me access to the private collection of Stan Cullis, particularly to his son Andrew and daughter Susan. Stan's nieces Rita Cullis and Dorothy Mason were also extremely helpful.

The affection and respect for Stan Cullis among people in the world of football is universal. That inspired me enormously. My thanks go especially to Jimmy Armfield, Ron Atkinson, Bryon Butler, Peter Creed, Doug Ellis, David Exall, John Giles, Bob Harris, Rachel Heyhoe-Flint, David Instone, Ken Jones, David Miller, Dr Neil Phillips, Bill Slater, Albert Stubbins, Graham Taylor, Walter Winterbottom and Kenneth Wolstenholme.

Chapter One

A Man of Honour

"...he is the passionate puritan..." John Arlott

STAN Cullis paused for thought as he stood proudly in the noisy bedlam of the Wolves dressing-room. His triumphant players had barely begun to wash off the mud and sweat from an extraordinary 3-2 victory over the crack Hungarian club team Honved. Cullis, a fiercely passionate and patriotic football manager, was surrounded by reporters demanding an instant reaction to the drama. He, in turn, was concerned to conjure up the appropriate words to convey what this night of sporting revenge meant to the people of England.

A few months earlier in 1954, the England national team had been humiliated 7-1 by Hungary in Budapest. The year before that England's long unbeaten home record had been shattered by a 6-3 defeat to the brilliant Magyars at Wembley. Six of the Hungarians, including the incomparable Ferenc Puskas, were playing for Honved that stormy winter night at the Molineux ground in Wolverhampton when lashing rain turned the pitch into a quagmire.

The match had a symbolic importance far beyond any rational reasoning of it. This was a victory that could allow the nation which invented football to believe it was once again a significant force. This was a victory to inspire a country still living with ration books and power cuts and choking fogs in its grey industrial cities. Cullis knew all this as he prepared to make an emphatic speech to the waiting newsmen who would send his words cascading round the globe.

"There they are, the champions of the world," said Cullis, pointing round to his exhausted and exhilarated players. "Champions of the world!"

He delivered the powerful sentence with total conviction – and changed the face of football forever. The boast by Cullis provoked an indignant reaction right across Europe, exactly as this most intelligent of managers must have known it would. It led directly to the birth of the European Cup a few months later, as the top continental clubs responded by setting up an official competition to discover which really was the champion team. Cullis was delighted. History sat comfortably on his broad shoulders and his bald head. He revelled in his role of repelling foreign invaders, and knew exactly the awesome effect that emotive words and phrases could generate. It is not an exaggeration to regard him as the Winston Churchill of English football.

That December night when the Wolves devoured Honved was the most treasured of his life. It is a truth evident in the private collection of mementoes that Cullis has kept from his mighty career in the game. Faded telegrams convey the reaction of a nation which watched with glowing pride as fluorescent gold shirts darted across fuzzy TV screens showing live pictures of the second half in which they scored three goals to recover from 2-0 down. From the high and mighty politicians and managers to the most humble fan, the victory against Honved and others like Spartak Moscow were a glorious inspiration.

"To the Manager, Wolverhampton Wanderers, Molyneux [*sic*] Ground. Congratulations, Wonderful Win Yesterday – Enoch Powell, House of Commons."

"To Stan Cullis. Strongly recommend unsatisfactory England team be scratched and glorious, magnificent, ferocious, goal-hungry Wolves substituted in entirety for important match against Germany – Merrett, Dolphin Hotel, Southampton."

"To Cullis, Football Club, Wolverhampton. Staff and boys of this school for cripple children offer warm congratulations on the Wolves magnificent vindication of British skill, character and guts on the football field – Headmaster Chailey Heritage Craft School, Sussex."

"To Molineux Football Club, Wolverhampton. Merry Christmas Wolves and thanks for kicking out the daylight of the continental teams. Carry on the good work – Friend, Luton."

"To Mr Stanley Cullis, Wanderers, Wolverhampton. Well done Stan. Good luck – Arthur Rowe, Manager, Tottenham Hotspur."

You may wonder what memories Stan Cullis holds of that magnificent night now that the European Champions League has become so dominant in football? You may wonder how he feels about the fall from grace of his beloved Wolves and their endless struggle to recapture the glories he routinely gave them?

Sadly, we cannot know. By the time this book was conceived it was too late to ask him to paint a picture of the many great matches and incidents of his career. His health and his memory are simply too frail. Living quietly and peacefully in a nursing home in the Malvern Hills, he cannot recall the past with any clarity.

The remarkable story of Stan Cullis must instead be pieced together from fragments, from the memories of others, from the newspaper archives, from his own private collection of letters and documents. It is the story of a boy who escaped from a grim childhood to become one of England's finest players, a majestic centre-half who was national team captain at the age of 22. It is the story of one of its greatest managers, a man whose fearsome reputation and leadership skills were allied to the sharpest of football brains. It is the story of a proud, decent and honourable Englishman. It is a story of secrets, the story of a man and a manager who was never given the credit he deserved by a game which in this country too quickly forgets and neglects its heroes.

Everyone had a view about Stan Cullis, complimentary or otherwise. The most accurate one-line assessment of him came in a phrase minted by John Arlott, who described Cullis as "the passionate puritan".

The passion underpinned his ferocious style of football management, it provided a steely suit of armour against a legion of critics who denigrated the so-called 'long-ball' tactics which lay at the heart of Wolverhampton's success through the 1950s. The passion for football was evident in everything he did. Cullis was a man so obsessed by the game that he once forgot he had taken his eleven-year-old son Andrew to a match and drove away from the ground alone after talking to old pals for two hours in the boardroom while the boy was still sitting patiently waiting for his famous father in a tea-room.

Great football managers have invariably been such single-minded men. What is essential to the story of Cullis, too, is the strong streak of puritanism in his character. He was a man of principle, a devout Christian. He never swore once in his life, not even during the most tyrannical half-time team-talk. The worst words that ever passed his lips when rage consumed him were 'flipping' or 'flopping'.

If the Honved victory is the enduring public image of the passionate Cullis, so the last game of his playing career in 1947 provides a vivid insight into the absolute integrity by which he lived his life. This side of his nature was kept intensely private, hidden not only from the gaze of curious fans, but very often even from those closest to him. It lies at the heart of his footballing life.

His final match was against Liverpool, an impossibly dramatic showdown for the Football League title. Wolves needed only a draw to be champions for the first time in their history, while opponents Liverpool knew they had to win the game on hostile territory to have a chance of taking the trophy instead.

Doctors had advised Cullis to stop playing a few months earlier after he had collapsed on a train while travelling home from a fixture at Middlesbrough. The specialist feared that continuing to head the heavy leather balls of the time might cause serious damage to his health, or even prove fatal. Cullis knew how precious was the glory of winning a first-ever League title for the club. So he compromised, taking a calculated risk of exposing his vulnerable skull to a few more matches through the winter and spring, but telling almost no-one of his dangerous gamble.

A few hours before the game against Liverpool, while the Wolves players were having lunch, Cullis suddenly stood up to make a speech. He stunned his team-mates by announcing this would be the last match of his career. One of his Wolves colleagues in that fixture against Liverpool was Billy Wright, later to win 105 international caps for England. "Stan's voice was choked with emotion and there were even tears in his eyes," recalled Wright later. "It was a huge surprise when he stood up to tell us it would be his final game. We all made up our minds nothing would stop us winning that match."

Before kick-off the psychological pressure was intensified still further. Cullis made another speech, this time addressing the crowd over the loudspeakers to make public his news. Molineux was momentarily dumbstruck. The voice of Cullis boomed on. He talked with emotion about his career, about losing in the FA Cup Final in 1939, and said here was his last chance of departing the stage with a winners' gold medal.

The atmosphere could not have been more highly charged on a blazing hot summer's day with the 50,765 crowd in their shirt-sleeves. Liverpool took an early lead and later in the first half had another great chance to score as a wonderful pass sent their centre-forward Albert Stubbins racing clear of the Wolves defence on goal. Chasing hard after him was Cullis, a centre-half capable of rugged, bone-shaking tackles. Cullis was no slouch for pace either, but Stubbins had three yards start and could not be caught with a fair tackle before he would shoot.

A Man of Honour

What emotions must have gone through the mind of Stan Cullis in those frozen moments when all the instincts and training of his life as a professional footballer came down to a split-second judgement? If he brought his opponent down with a foul tackle Wolves would stay just a goal away from winning the title that Cullis, his team-mates, the noisy crowd, and the whole town craved. If he let Stubbins go the talented centre-forward was almost certain to score the goal which would surely take the title to Liverpool.

The passion for winning and his hatred of losing was set against what Cullis knew absolutely to be right and wrong. And he simply could not bring himself to foul Stubbins as the centre-forward sprinted ahead on the Molineux turf. It would have been a betrayal of all he believed in, a betrayal of his own soul.

Stubbins raced on and scored to make it 2-0. Wolves rallied gallantly after half-time, clawed one goal back, but Liverpool clung on for a 2-1 victory which gave them the spoils. The honesty of Cullis had lost the game for Wolves.

"I remember getting a head start on Stan," recalls Stubbins. "But all he had to do was pull my jersey and he'd have stopped me in my tracks. I could hear him behind me, but he was too big a man to stoop to that kind of tactic, even though in those days he probably wouldn't even have been booked, never mind sent off. It turned out to be the vital moment of the match, and I vividly remember going up to shake his hand at the final whistle and seeing that he was crying. There were tears in his eyes, and I can assure you he wasn't hamming it up. He wasn't that kind of man. He was a hard footballer, an England captain, and it was an indication of just how much it had meant to him.

"Other players would certainly have fouled me that day. But not Stan. We had some real tough battles on the park, but we never fouled each other. I believe that he has been asked many times since why he didn't tug my jersey, and always it's the same answer. He couldn't bring himself to do it. I admired him for that, I really did."

If Cullis ever felt a moment of regret about his refusal to foul Stubbins he never said so in public, nor even privately to his son Andrew in many hours of conversation about football. When he wrote a book *All For The Wolves*, in 1960, he described in detail his fears about the head injury, but skated over that fateful final match of his career, making no mention of his great moral dilemma. "At one stage Wolves held a lead of eleven points, but frost and snow settled on England and we did not play a match for five weeks," he recalled. "The Government, in these years of hard work after the War, asked football authorities not to arrange midweek matches which might draw people away from the factories. So the season dragged on until the early days of June, and Wolves lost not only their rhythm, but their lead in the Championship too. Eventually we finished a point behind Liverpool, the champions, and behind Manchester United on goal average as well."

The incident was a closed book in his mind as Cullis forged a new career as the most feared manager, and one of the most successful, in football. What was a lost match and a lost trophy in the first League season after a world war that claimed so many millions of lives? It wasn't so hard in the summer of 1947 to keep sporting action in perspective. Not for a man of principle, anyway.

There are so many facets to Stan Cullis, so many myths that surround him. Some mention the puritan streak to his character and say he was a teetotaller. That isn't true. He drank in strict moderation only, but his particular tipple was cider. In later years he has enjoyed a glass or two of wine. A pint of beer was extremely rare, but after matches he would relish the chance to talk football in the local pubs with other managers like Matt Busby or Bill Shankly. He smoked too, although again not to excess. Son Andrew and some of the Wolves players are convinced that habit began entirely as a means of combating the tension and stress of football management.

Another myth is that he was a hard-hearted and ruthless character loathed by the players whom he bullied with a searing tongue. The sobriquet Cullis was given by the popular press was the 'Iron Manager'. Of course, to an extent, the players lived and worked in fear of a man who was very definitely The Boss. Dennis Wilshaw, an England centre-forward and Molineux hero of the time, said recently: "I think the team spirit in the Wolves side stemmed from the fact that we all hated his guts. Maybe that's a bit severe, but we were all united because we felt the same about the manager."

They shared the trepidation – and they shared the respect. In the family collection there is a letter Wilshaw wrote to Cullis the day after he was sacked as Wolves manager in September 1964. It says: "No-one could have done more for Wolves. You have helped me and many more like me to a happy career in the game, and your dedication, honesty and high character have made a profound mark upon my life. I am proud that I have worked with you for, I like to think, your standards have become my standards."

Wilshaw's team-mate Billy Wright said that Cullis had a "Jekyll and Hyde character" as a manager. The public and the fans knew all about the intense Saturday afternoon figure who barked his sergeant major orders on the touchline, but little about the "cool, rational and immensely approachable" man that Wright found him to be during the week when his office door was always open.

The callous sacking of Cullis is another defining moment in the history of English football; it was the first time a truly big-name manager had been dismissed by a panicking board of directors, and it set a pattern which has been endlessly repeated. None, perhaps, has ever had quite the same shocking impact. Cullis was The Wolves. He had joined the club as a teenage apprentice in 1934, become first-team captain in the week of his twentieth birthday, and as a manager brought them unprecedented success – three League titles, two FA Cups and a collection of famous friendly victories against exotic visitors like Moscow Spartak, Real Madrid and Honved. In the weeks prior to his sacking Cullis had been unwell, an illness which the benefit of hindsight tells us was perhaps the first of several mini-strokes he has suffered.

The decision by the Wolves board of directors provoked another blizzard of mail through the letter-box of the Cullis home in a smart suburb of Wolverhampton. A handwritten note penned the next day by his most valued friend in football, Matt Busby, a rival manager with Manchester United, was also kept by Cullis. It reads:

16th Sept 1964.

My Dear Stan,

I am still trying to recover from the shock of yesterday's announcement. It has knocked me sick of human nature. How people could do such a thing after you giving them your life's blood? What more success can they get than what you've given them? What loyalty have they shown you after the loyalty you have given them in every way? Oh, I could go on and on. Anyway, Stan, please accept my sincere sympathies, and whatever you decide to do in the future may it abound with happiness and success in the wish of

Your Friend,

Matt.

Busby knew Cullis better than almost anyone. He knew the honour and integrity of his friend, and this informs the truly shocking tone of distress in Busby's letter.

The honesty of Stan Cullis was unimpeachable. One day he found a spare couple of hours to watch his son, then nine years old, playing in a boys' league match in Wolverhampton. "I was so thrilled that he turned up," remembered Cullis junior. "He never had the time to watch me with all his commitments at the Wolves. My team won 5-1 and I scored a hat-trick. I felt so pleased, you can imagine my delight. Then, as I walked off the pitch, he came over to me and his first words were, 'No, son, you'll never make it.' What a thing it was to say, but that was my father. He was very straight. He couldn't tell you anything but what he knew to be the truth."

The little boy had dreamed until then of growing up to be a centre-forward for the Wolves. He became, much to his father's joy, the Reverend Andrew Cullis.

Chapter Two

Iron in the Soul

"...he had been playing only a few minutes before I realised I was watching a lad who was destined to go a long way..." Major Frank Buckley

THE headline writers who christened Stan Cullis with the title of 'The Iron Manager' did so to reflect the image of the man whose imposing character and white-hot determination forged the outstanding Wolves team of the 1950s. It was wholly appropriate for another reason, however.

Stan Cullis grew up in the industrial town of Ellesmere Port on the Wirral. The Cullis family had moved there from Wolverhampton many years before Stanley, the youngest of ten children, was born on 25 October 1916. It was a forced relocation because Stan's father was employed by the Wolverhampton Corrugated Iron Company, which moved north lock, stock and barrel for economic reasons. The area round their factory, the streets of endless two-up, two-down terraced houses where Stan lived as a child, became known as 'little Wolverhampton'. He lived at No. 60 Oldfields Road, which survives today, and looks much as it must have done 85 years ago. Some houses are boarded up, others lovingly renovated. Round the corner is the church which became a focus of young Stan's existence.

When Stan was a boy, learning his football on these deprived streets, his family life was far from easy. His mother, Elizabeth, was an invalid who was confined to a wheelchair due to polio. She rarely left the living room of the tiny house. His father, Billy, was an old man by the time his last child was born and relied almost totally on his sons to provide the family income.

Throughout his life Stan rarely spoke to anyone about his childhood, even his own children. His niece, Rita Cullis, who is a singer with the English National Opera, and who grew up in Ellesmere Port, is one of few surviving family members with any knowledge of those days.

She said: "The ten children, including my father Sydney, came from a very tough background. He told me they were so poor the children wore clogs. If the clogs needed mending they didn't go to school that day. The next day would be awful because the headmaster would haul them up in front of the whole school to demand an explanation. It must have been a humiliating experience.

"Their mother was in a wheelchair. She would sit in the chair in the living room the whole day just tapping her fingers on the arm of the chair and it would drive them all barmy. Stan's father would often be seen sitting alone on the steps of the Catholic church just to get away from the home."

Young Stan had three escape valves from this bleak house; playing football in the cobbled yard between the grey houses at the back of Oldfields Road, going to church, and trying to educate himself at the Cambridge Road school and later at night classes when his father refused to let him go to grammar school.

One of the few stories Cullis told his son Andrew about his early life was that of an angry confrontation in the house between his ageing father Billy and the headmaster of the Cambridge Road school. Andrew recalled: "I never heard my father speak ill of many people, except his own dad, who was a very difficult character. The headmaster of the local primary school came to see him and said: 'Oh I think Stan should go to the grammar school', and his father said 'No'. There was a blazing argument between the headmaster and him, but there was no way Stan's father would back down. He wanted his son to go out to work and earn money for the family."

This is confirmed by Rita Cullis, who said: "He didn't let any of the children go to grammar school, even though Sydney and Stan were certainly bright enough to do so. It caused huge arguments. He wanted the children to earn money to bring into the house because both Stan's parents were very old by then. My father went to work in an iron foundry rather than carry on his schooling as he wanted to. He told me it was so hot in the factory that if a piece of paper fell on the floor it burned instantly. Stan was too young to go there before he joined the Wolves, but he and my father both studied at night school in the hope of building a better life."

It is impossible to know whether Stan Cullis would have ended up labouring in the ironworks if he had not become a professional footballer, but it is a reasonable supposition to make given the environment he lived in. That was the major form of employment in the area.

We will never know, either, whether one of Stan's elder brothers, Arthur, might have made the grade as a professional footballer too. Dorothy Mason, the daughter of Stan's elder sister, Ethel, explained: "Everyone in the family thought that Arthur was a better footballer even than Stan. As a youngster he was being sought after by a number of clubs, but had a dreadful accident at the steel mill where he worked. A piece of machinery severed his foot and of course that was the end of of his chance to play football."

At one stage, probably before Stan was born, his father also worked in the soap factory at Port Sunlight on the Wirral. The Cullis family were offered one of the houses in the model town built to provide a more comfortable existence for the working class man and his family. Billy Cullis rejected the offer; he wanted to stay living in his 'little Wolverhampton' district of Ellesmere Port, however cramped and demeaning the conditions.

Billy Cullis's native affection for Wolverhampton, little did he know it at the time, was to have a profound affect on the history of the town he loved. So, probably, did his stubborn rejection of the chance for his son Stan to attend the grammar school where he might have taken up rugby and cricket.

Instead, young Stan kicked a ball around the yard in the time when he wasn't studying at night school or working as an errand boy and shop assistant for Dyson's the grocers, where his elder sister Ethel also worked. As with so many footballers of his time he developed naturally, without a hint of coaching, the skills that would provide his path to a new life. We can be fairly certain, as well, that the soccer played by these working class kids would have been ferociously hard. Stan would have learned to look after himself physically.

One of the boys he played with, by remarkable coincidence, was Joe Mercer, who also became a celebrated footballer; an England international alongside Cullis and later a rival manager in the First Division. Mercer recalled that time with a clear rather than sentimental eye, saying years later: "Back alley football is only a substitute for the real thing. We always have to fight for bigger and better playing fields for children. But, all the same, the back alleys did hold some valuable lessons of their own. For instance, playing with a small ball. If you could control a small ball with certainty, you found later that bringing down a normal ball came more easily. It was wonderful training for the eye." Both Mercer and Cullis became highly skilful professional footballers.

Mercer also worked for Dyson's, attended the Cambridge Road School, and lived a few streets away from the Cullis home. Stan's son Andrew said: "My father and Joe played in the same school team. Joe was centre-forward and my dad inside-forward. My dad scored a goal, and as they walked back to the centre-circle Joe turned to him and said 'you shouldn't have done that, I'm the centre-forward, I'm meant to score the goals'. They were great friends."

At that time the town of Ellesmere Port was split into two distinct camps. Mercer was from a local family, one of the 'Portites', and there was a friendly rivalry with the boys who were sons of the immigrants from Wolverhampton, the 'Wafflers'. Cullis recalled the atmosphere, saying: "There existed a division among the population, a mild cold shoulder was quite evident with the unwelcome attitude arising on the part of the Portites towards the migrant Midlanders."

That rivalry must have been part of the street football scene, too, where the children would mostly use bundles of newspaper wrapped in string for their ball. Occasionally, there might be the luxury of kicking a tennis ball around. Other hobbies of the youngsters were traditional activities like scrumping apples and diving into the Manchester Ship Canal from bridges, especially on cold days near the steelworks where the water expelled from the factory was enticingly hot.

Another boy from the area, too, was Frank Soo, who had a fine career with Stoke City and also played wartime internationals for England. It was obviously a classic football breeding ground, and you have to wonder whether the instinctive competition among such talented boys helped to improve their skills even further. They would all have wanted to be the best.

There were, however, many avenues that the teenage Cullis considered before football captured his soul forever. He took a course in book-keeping in the hope it might lead to accountancy, a respectable and well-paid career. He learned how to write in shorthand because the thrill of journalism also appealed. He made swift progress learning French and Esperanto, at a time when there was a widespread belief that the universal language would be adopted around the world; his brother Sydney also became fluent in Esperanto. It is quite clear that playing professional football was only one option among many as Stan grew up in Ellesmere Port.

Even today, when much of his memory has been lost, Stan Cullis can still speak Esperanto. His son Andrew said: "My father remembers that better than anything else, even than what he may just have eaten for lunch. The staff in his nursing home will fall about laughing at it. They occasionally ask him to speak in Esperanto and he regales them with whole paragraphs that he learnt 70-odd years ago. It is quite extraordinary really. But he was very keen to get as much education as he could, and I suppose it shows how determined he was to make something of himself."

Stan Cullis – The Iron Manager

When Stan Cullis became the great manager he was, several characteristics marked him out; intensity, determination, a relentless work ethic, a fierce contempt for slackers, a sympathy for young players with domestic problems, and a driving puritanism. All of these elements of his nature, it seems to me, can be traced back to his formative years in Ellesmere Port.

A huge influence on the young Stan Cullis was religion. Whitby Methodist church was situated just behind his house and that became one alternative home. So did St Thomas's church, round the corner from Oldfields Road, where the boy was sent to Sunday school mainly as a device to get him out of an overcrowded house for a few hours. Stan found he enjoyed the life there; perhaps it provided a vivid contrast to the uneasy atmosphere within his family home.

The church provided both a moral education and a social life. Stan played tennis at the Methodist church club, enjoying that as much as his football, and excelling thanks to his natural capacity for ball skills. The clearest personal indication Cullis gave of how formative this experience had been was in a newspaper article years later when asked about his famous refusal to use bad language. It was his most single famous character trait, a fact which everyone mentions when they talk about the Iron Manager.

"I never used bad language to the players," remembered Cullis. "At the age of eleven I decided never to swear. I take no great credit for this. I know many men of integrity and standing in the community who swear. Their reputation is not lessened by it. It is simply that I dislike swearing." At the age of eleven, playing football on some of the roughest back alleys in England, it seems most likely that this stern choice was prompted by his immersion in church life.

His son Andrew, who became a vicar himself, is convinced this religious background had a profound influence on the way his father lived his life and the way he managed the Wolverhampton Wanderers team. He explained: "There was a strong moral sense of what was right and wrong in the family home as I grew up. I'm sure that my father's faith comes from his young days.

"He was very strong and principled. very Christian. There was a strong work ethic that I feel certain was a result of his childhood experience. He was always intelligent and he was a lot more intellectual than football life allowed. He never really developed fully in that sphere of life, but he has become nicer and gentler in his old age than when my sister and I were children.

"I remember an incident from my childhood on my seventh birthday. There were many cards up on the mantlepiece at home and my father came in and asked who they were for. He had no idea at all that it was my birthday. I remember, too, that he never sent a birthday card or Christmas card or anything like that. I'm sure that is because his family were too poor to send cards. They never did – and it never occurred to him that's what you did.

"He wasn't even sure on which day and in which year he was born. I have seen various versions in books and articles, but 25 October 1916 is on the birth certificate. Within our family, birthdays and Christmases just passed him by. Perhaps it also explains something about what his childhood was like. My father said very little about his family. I had the impression that he didn't want to."

The reason for the reticence is unclear, but was probably to do with nothing more than the obsessive nature of life as a top football manager. Even his own family life took second place most of the time to working for the Wolves. Stan was certainly proud of his roots in Ellesmere Port, returning when he could to visit his childhood home. In 1949, for instance, he took the FA Cup itself to 60 Oldfields Road to show his father Billy the first trophy Wolves had won for half a century. What a stir that must have caused among the Wafflers of Ellesmere Port.

Niece Dorothy Mason, who still lives in the area, recalled the day, saying: "Stan arrived with the Cup and some of the Wolves players. He took it into the house to show Granny Cullis in her wheelchair. He never forgot where he came from. I remember too that his England caps were kept at his parents house for many years. I always liked to wear them when I was a small girl visiting. He also used to bring presents home from his foreign trips like the one to Romania where he was England captain. All the family were so proud of his achievements."

Rita Cullis remembered how Joe Mercer and Stan returned on a joint visit to officially open a new football clubhouse in the town. "Stan was keenly aware of where he came from," she said: "even though he rarely went back once he was famous at the Wolves."

Stan's brothers Billy and Sydney both did scouting work for Wolves in the Ellesmere Port area. Rita explained: "My father wasn't paid, he just did it out of loyalty to his brother. He would drive anywhere for Stan to watch a match where there might be a youngster who Wolves had become interested in. They were very close, and the family were so proud of Stan's success in football. I went with my father to watch many matches at Molineux."

For all his extra-curricular studies and his happiness in the church environment, it was always going to be football that would provide Stan Cullis with the best chance of escape from his difficult childhood. The earliest picture of him is one he kept in his collection – a photograph of the Ellesmere Port schoolboys team that played against Chester Boys in January 1929. Stan was aged twelve at the time, and is down on the list of names as first reserve.

He wasn't often left out of the team, and at ten years old he captained his Cambridge Road School football side. Maybe he was the best player in the team, or maybe the schoolmaster who organised the side recognised leadership qualities in the young Cullis. A year later Stan was playing for the town team – Ellesmere Port Wednesday, so named because all the shops closed on a Wednesday and people could play football that afternoon. It was with them that he won his first honour in football, a runners'-up medal in the Liverpool Hospital Cup. Wednesday had reached the Final played at Anfield.

Who were his early influences? Certainly, there was Joe Mercer, who was a year older than Cullis and a step ahead of him on the path to fame. He won an apprentice contract at Everton. The footballer Cullis admired most was Matt Busby of Manchester City and Scotland. Busby was a wing-half, the position Cullis was growing into, and he said: "As a youth in Ellesmere Port, as often as I could I would go and watch Busby play and try to model myself on him." Years later the pair would become the greatest of friends and the greatest of playing and managerial opponents.

A key figure as well was teacher Bill Roberts, a young man who arrived from North Wales. Unlike most of the strict, stand-offish schoolmasters Roberts would actually join his pupils in their street football games, playing on the weaker side. He organised the school team and practice matches on local works grounds or the Ellesmere Port Wednesday pitch itself. Mercer and Cullis both learnt much about football in this fortunate set-up and began to be noticed by the scouts employed by leading football clubs.

Mercer went to a local club in Everton, while Cullis's case was taken up by a prominent Merseyside sportsman, Tom Corley, who began trying to interest teams in the talented grocer's boy from Ellesmere Port. There was, initially at least, a distinct lack of enthusiasm for this youngster. Stan did sign amateur forms for Bolton Wanderers in 1933, but one trial match brought a swift end to hopes of a professional contract. Cullis was considered too slow. The history of football is littered with such errors of judgement.

The next offer of a trial came from Wolves, but there is a fascinating difference of opinions about how that arose. In his book *All For The Wolves*, Stan Cullis wrote that his father had insisted from an early age that the only club he would allow his son to join was Wolverhampton Wanderers, his home-town team. The trial with Bolton had "only been a concession to allow me to gain experience", said Cullis. According to this version of events it was a Football League referee, Mr Joe Forshaw, who lived in Ellesmere Port, who recommended the teenager to Wolves' famous manager, Major Frank Buckley.

However, Buckley himself in two ghosted newspaper columns many years apart, both kept by Stan Cullis in his collection, gives a different view. He explained how Wolves in the 1930s were inundated with letters telling them to look out for this or that talented young boy.

"I particularly remember one Wolves supporter," wrote Buckley, "a man whose family had lived in the town for generations. He had moved to Cheshire, but he wrote to me and said he thought his son had the makings of a fine footballer, and would I give him a trial for the "Wafflers" – the local name for the team. Well, I took a chance and gave the lad a trial. It was one of the few chances that turn out to be a winner. He had been playing only a few minutes before I realised I was watching a lad who was destined to go a long way. I looked at his name: Stanley Cullis."

Stan's son Andrew has a little more to add. From conversations with his father he believes that a number of other leading teams had become interested in signing up the tough, skilful wing-half of Ellesmere Port Wednesday, maybe in response to the side's progress to the Hospital Cup Final at Anfield. That was surely likely to have been the case for a lad who would go on to captain England.

"Liverpool and other clubs were keen to sign him," said Andrew. "But his father was adamant that it should be Wolves."

There is no doubt that Billy Cullis desperately wanted his son to play for the 'Wafflers', and despite all the problems surrounding the family that desire is likely to have had a profound influence on Stan. In Wolverhampton, also, he could live with his Aunt, which would give the teenager an immediate sense of belonging. If he had joined a local club like Liverpool, Stan would probably have continued living in Oldfields Road. That may not have been such an enticing prospect for an ambitious seventeen-year-old.

Yet another version is given by Doug Ellis, the current Aston Villa chairman, who also grew up in the area a few years later than Mercer and Cullis. He said: "The man who made it all possible was Billy Roberts, who worked so hard on schools football in the area. He was a great man and it was he, I believe, who got Stan the chance to go to Molineux."

The exact truth behind the way Stan Cullis joined the Wolves and began a thirty-year connection with Molineux that changed the face of football will remain unknown. Perhaps both Joe Forshaw and Billy Cullis wrote letters to Buckley. Perhaps the influence of Bill Roberts was the key factor.

It was certainly a fateful decision that Buckley made to employ the ambitious, dedicated and enthusiastic lad from Ellesmere Port with iron in his soul.

Chapter Three

Passport to Success

"...he was the most classical centre-half of his time..." Ferenc Puskas

THE future England captain arrived at his Aunt Ginny's house in Wolverhampton on 10 February 1934. He had travelled light on the train from Ellesmere Port, wearing the only pair of trousers he owned, and armed with the few other clothes he possessed, a pair of football boots, and a letter that informed he would be paid a weekly salary of two pounds and ten shillings plus a win bonus of five shillings if the Wolves 'A' team won their Saturday match in the Birmingham Combination.

"I felt on top of the world," he remembered later.

Professional football was not only a passport to a prosperous and glamorous new life; it was also a happy escape from all the traumas of his childhood existence. This, surely, explains the fierce dedication Stan Cullis brought to his formative year at Molineux, an intensity of purpose which Major Buckley quickly realised set this particular boy apart from the many teenagers he signed for the Wolves in his seventeen years as manager of the club. In the photographs which survive from those early days his face has the look of an innocent church choirboy. Opponents quickly discovered the iron in his boots.

Stan began in the 'A' team as a wing-half, and within two months had been made the skipper. Before the end of the season Buckley called the youth into his office and told him: "Cullis, if you listen and do as you are told, I will make you the captain of Wolves." Buckley remembered the time with understandable pride many years later when the boy had not only become club skipper, but succeeded him as the manager too. "Even in those junior days it was apparent that he knew what he wanted," said Buckley. "What he wanted was football fame – and he was determined to get it. He set out to master the secrets of his chosen profession. Nothing short of England's captaincy was his goal, and he responded with alacrity to coaching and advice. Cullis had to work his way up through the Central League side, but once he had made the first team there was no other place for him."

His contract with Wolves, put on display at the Football Hall of Fame in central London, was full of homilies to the young men like Cullis who arrived dreaming of glory. The tone immediately puts them in their place as servants of The Club.

1) The player hereby agrees to play in an efficient manner and to the best of his ability for The Club.

2) The player shall attend The Club's ground or any other place decided upon by The Club for the purpose of training as a player to the instructions of the secretary, manager or trainer. (This provision does not apply if players employed by The Club are paid a weekly wage of less than One Pound.)

3) The player shall do everything possible to keep himself in the best possible condition so as to render the most efficient service to The Club and will carry out all training and other instructions of The Club through its representative officials.

For the months from February 1934 through to that summer young Stan excelled in what was effectively the Wolves third XI. He returned to Ellesmere Port for a few weeks in June, but was then summoned back to Molineux halfway through the close season by Buckley, who was intent on ensuring his protege kept his feet on the ground. "The Major informed me that I was to be the groundsman's assistant," recalled Cullis. "So I, a fully fledged professional who had been told he would be captain of Wolves one day, found myself weeding the pitch, pulling the roller and laying seed in company with the lads on the ground staff. There wasn't much chance of me becoming full of my own importance, and my ego didn't last long under Major Buckley." An understanding of the many facets of a football club did.

That summer, too, the strength of Cullis's character was tested when he conducted the first wage negotiations of his career. He was offered a contract for the next season on the same financial terms, two pounds and ten shillings, even though he had become captain of the 'A' side. The seventeen-year-old demanded a rise of ten shillings to three pounds per week, and when it was bluntly rejected he decided to call the bluff of the club by declaring he would return home to Ellesmere Port. It was the last place on earth he must have wanted to go, especially knowing that he might perhaps be out of work and facing life on the dole at a time of deep economic recession. At the least his income would be severely reduced. But for Stan Cullis justice had to be done, and had to be seen to be done.

He went to collect his boots from the dressing-room, but was told to wait by Jack Davies, the first-team trainer, who intervened on behalf of the talented young footballer. The lad was called to a meeting with the manager and one of the Wolves directors, Ben Matthews, who tried to intimidate the youth by warning him of the dire consequences of his actions. "Mr Matthews, I shall not starve," said Cullis. "I was living before I came to Wolves and no doubt I shall go on living after I leave Wolves." Moral courage earned the player his pay rise, and no doubt added respect from Buckley. By 1939 Cullis's pay had risen to £7 per week during the season, £6 in the summer, plus £1 appearance money.

All that time he continued to travel home to the family house in Ellesmere Port to live during the summer break. Much of the time was spent with his young equal, Joe Mercer. Cullis said: "There was a unique similarity about the life of Joe and myself, which almost seemed the work of a scriptwriter. He was a person of impeccable honesty and whose friendship you treasured. In the summer break when I went home to my parents at Ellesmere Port I played golf with Joe at the Hooton Golf Club. I rarely finished on the winning side."

Cullis shared the honesty of Mercer, and the moral courage he possessed also earned him swift promotion through the ranks when he displayed that character trait on the field. In the new season he began to play in the reserves, still as a wing-half, and after his eighteenth birthday became the captain of that team as well. In a Central League match at Blackpool another of the directors ordered that the inside-forwards switch positions during the game. Cullis immediately countermanded the move, and told the director in the dressing-room afterwards that, as captain, he gave the orders out on the pitch. Buckley happily backed the young man who appeared to be a natural born leader.

One of the most vital matches of Stan's career was a practice game one Tuesday morning, staged for the benefit of Dave 'Boy' Martin, an Irish centre-forward Wolves had signed for a large transfer fee. Due to injuries there was no centre-half available, and Cullis was asked to fill the role as an emergency measure. The teenager, out of position, played Martin off the park in this private game watched only by Wolves officials. 'What about our new forward, then?' asked one of the directors to Major Buckley. 'What about our new centre-half!' was the manager's instant reply. Cullis rarely played in any other position again.

A few weeks later, on 16 February 1935, barely a year after arriving at his aunt's house, Stan was given his first-team debut for the Wolves at home to Huddersfield. The local *Express and Star* paper had a short item to that effect, saying: "Cullis played in the A and Central League teams last season, and has been showing improved form in recent weeks with the reserve team. He is not yet twenty years of age." That faded cutting remains in Cullis's collection among reports of many more fabled football incidents. The match was lost 3-2 at Molineux; Wolves, fifth from bottom of the table, being outclassed by the visitors. Centre-forward Martin had a poor game, but a report in the *Sporting Star* said: "Cullis opened well and showed promise occasionally." He stayed in the first team for two further games, and was then summarily demoted back to the third team the following Saturday to keep life in perspective.

That kind of harsh lesson was well learnt by Cullis, who practised similar psychology himself when he became a manager. If justice was a prevailing theme of his footballing career, so was an obsessive desire for education. That continued mainly in the Central League until October 1936, when a vivid performance against England and Everton centre-forward Dixie Dean signalled the final breakthrough as a professional sportsman.

Wolves' regular first-team centre-half had been William Morris, but he was switched to full-back for this match to cover an injury. Cullis was promoted up from the reserves, and matched the great Dean blow for blow through a fixture Everton won by a single goal. The performance was witnessed by Dr Percy Young, who later became a great friend of Cullis and wrote a history of the club. He recalled: "With abundant energy the newcomer opposed the Everton centre-forward, and the resultant clash of contrasting temperaments called for some friendly advice to both players from the referee." It would not be the last time Stan's passion for the game fell foul of the authorities, nor the last he had titanic physical struggles with the powerful centre-forwards of the day.

Morris stayed at right-back, and Cullis remained at centre-half. They would be England international team-mates three times as well in those positions. Stan was still not nineteen years old, yet within another year of phenomenal progress he would be the official club captain of the Wolves.

What kind of player was he? Every description begins with his trademark crouching movement, his balding head thrust forward, his elbows and arms pumping at his side to keep opponents at bay. He was mentally strong and alert, blessed with immense powers of concentration on the ball, on opponents, and on the strategy of a match. He could pass accurately, tackle ferociously, and many of those who played against him talk of his incredible coolness under pressure; he never seemed hurried or flustered in possession of the ball. His native intelligence was backed up by hard work; Cullis kept a private book about all the centre-forwards he ever played against, noting down their strengths and weaknesses. He has also been described as the last of the old attacking centre-halves, a man who wanted to be the complete footballer, who could both attack and defend, a man who could not bear to waste a pass.

Dennis Wilshaw, who played in a wartime match as a team-mate of Cullis when he was just sixteen years old and who later became an England international and a Wolves regular in the 1950s, recalled: "He was a brilliant ball player. What mystified me was the way he used to pull the ball down in a defensive position and do a little shimmy-shammy with it. When he was a manager he would never let us do anything like that."

Perfection is impossible. However much Cullis loved to attack, however great a ballplayer he was, the curious fact was that he never scored a League or Cup goal for the Wolves throughout his career in an age when high-scoring matches were commonplace.

The testimony of men who played against him is the most reliable witness to his place in football's pantheon. It leaves no room for doubt. "A forward needed the penetrative powers of a tank and the pace of a racing whippet to get past Cullis," said Tommy Lawton, among the most accomplished centre-forwards to wear an England shirt. "He was the best centre-half I ever played against. He was strong and upright in a tackle and was constantly heading the ball away. When he received the ball on the ground his arms would start working like flippers as he started an elegant run upfield or played a pass of such precision that the angles seemed to be calculated as if using a set-square."

Ferenc Puskas, the incomparable Hungarian genius, said simply: "Cullis was the most classical centre-half of his time anywhere in the world."

Ron Greenwood, widely regarded as one of the most intelligent men in the history of English football, who for a spell was the national team manager, said this: "Cullis combined art and conflict in the twin roles of a centre-half. He would not accept for a moment that a centre-half should simply be an agent of destruction. He was a student of football. He had that kind of mind, always challenging and always broadening his knowledge. When I was at Chelsea as a player, Billy Birrell, the manager, told me to go and watch Cullis every time he came to London. 'You'll never be as good as Cullis,' he said. 'But I want you to watch the way he plays.'

"Stanley had an unmistakeable crouching style, with arms and elbows working, and this made it very difficult for opponents to get near him. I remember playing against him in the war as a seventeen-year-old when he guested for Aldershot and they had a famous half-back line of Mercer, Cullis and Britton. They made an indelible impression on me – but Cullis most of all. There was one memorable moment when he found himself with the ball at his feet on his own goal-line, just outside the penalty area and facing the crowd. One of our team, an international called Smith, a good player, moved right up behind him and there seemed no way Cullis could escape. But, still facing the crowd, his back to Smith, he started selling dummies to a man he couldn't see. His body went this way and that, the ball untouched, until he suddenly moved – the ball went with him – and Smith was left facing the crowd all by himself."

Stan Mortensen, an England centre-forward, enjoyed many battles against Cullis, and liked the fact that he gave opponents a chance by attempting tricks in dangerous areas of the field. He said: "For many people Cullis was a centre-half above all others. He had a willingness to take a risk holding ball in his own area and then dribble up field. He certainly had astute captaincy and was an outstanding player, although people will argue whether it was all for the best."

Goalkeepers who played in the same team would often be left at their wits end watching his fancy-dan tricks in his own penalty box. As a manager Cullis became famous worldwide for his advocacy of the long-ball style. As a player he resolutely refused to resort to an agricultural hoof upfield to clear his lines. It is another curiosity of his character. Wolves' celebrated goalkeeper Bert Williams recalled: "Stan would pass a foot over the ball, first one way, then another. His body always seemed to be going in the opposite direction and even though I knew his game I found it difficult to read him."

Frank Swift, England's keeper, said: "There was no other player in the game I would allow to play so much football in the area as Stan Cullis. He was one of the most controversial centre-halves. Half the people who watched him disliked him, the other half worshipped him. He would goad you as a player. In the dressing-room before games he would stand in front of the mirror and spend several minutes trying to part his hair to cover his bald patch. He must have tried every hair restorer known to man."

The vanity about his baldness came later. As a young player before the war Cullis made his reputation as a player of unyielding vigour. He did not resort to sly or snide fouls, but few matched his ferocity in the tackle, and it led to many clashes with opposing centre-forwards, more than a few of whom would try to intimidate the young man by punching him off the ball. On occasions Cullis was knocked out, but he never retreated as a result. In fact, the moral indignation it provoked made him an even more formidable opponent.

Later in 1936 Major Buckley tried to sign a second Stan for the Wolves. Unfortunately, the attempt to purchase Stanley Matthews was rejected by Stoke City. Cullis and Matthews had to be content to share a field as England players before and during the Second World War, the Wizard of Dribble saying of his colleague: "Cullis was a fine attacking centre-half and a sound captain. He knew what he intended to do, and would come out of a ruck of players from defence with his arms out and his demeanour full of authority."

It would be in the 1937-38 season that Cullis began to be considered as a regular international player himself. The *Morning Post* report of a match between Chelsea and Wolves said: "England selectors who saw the Wolves win 2-0 at Stamford Bridge must have been convinced that they had also seen the most accomplished centre-half in the country in Stan Cullis. He mastered the centre-forward and still found time to play the part of the complete general."

Cullis had occasionally been skipper of the Wolves' first team when he was still nineteen years old. It was not until the week of his twentieth birthday, in October 1936, that even Buckley, the great champion of teenagers, was prepared to hand him the official club captaincy. Stan admitted many years later that "I had been horrified when the Major first said I would be the captain. I was still worried about keeping my place in the side as a youngster. But whatever I was involved in, I always seemed to end up as a captain, whether it was cricket and football at school or if I'd decided to take up tennis and golf. Some people don't relish the responsibility but it didn't bother me at all. In fact I liked it, even when Sir Stanley Rous reminded me when I was England captain that I was responsible not only for my own actions on the field but also those of my teammates."

One of the first games after that was a home clash against Chelsea. Wolves lost 2-1 and a section of the Molineux crowd angrily invaded the pitch and broke the goalposts at both ends of the ground. Hooligan behaviour has a long history in English football.

In the four previous seasons Wolves had finished 20th, 15th, 17th and 15th respectively in the First Division table after being promoted from the Second Division in the 1931-32 season. A reputation for being makeweights was justified. With Cullis as captain they finished fifth, second and second in the three years before war broke out.

The influence of the inspirational new skipper was profound, far more so than the constant innovations which Major Buckley brought to Molineux to try to find an edge over rival clubs. He was the first manager, for example, to investigate the use of a sporting psychologist. Cullis recalled: "That created something of a sensation. I attended the psychologist's surgery in Wolverhampton on some half dozen occasions. So far as I could gather he tried to build up my confidence through an analysis of my problems and worries which, at this stage of my career, were not very many."

Various gadgets with wonderfully pseudo-scientific titles were carted into a dressing-room of sceptical players. There was a therapeutic diathermy machine, a universal machine for galvanism, sumsoidal and paradic treatments, and a machine which gave out ultra-violet rays for irradiation.

Most controversially, there was the infamous monkey gland episode. The Wolves players were injected by hypodermic syringe with what Buckley told the world were 'animal secretions'. The theory was that monkey gland injections would help his footballers to grow stronger and taller, and their use created an inevitable uproar long before the days of track and field athletes taking anabolic steroids to artificially boost performances. In 1938 the FA held an inquiry into "the idea of pumping extracts of animals into footballers" and announced that "players were at liberty to decide for themselves whether or not they have the injections." Inside forward Dickie Dorsett was the only player who flatly refused to have the treatment, but many others gave it up long before the end because they felt it had no practical effect.

Billy Wright, a teenage recruit, was too junior to have the injections. He was given foul-tasting brown tablets to take instead, and admitted years later that he often gave them to his landlady's cat, "who did very well on them." Cullis himself believed it was mainly a publicity stunt by the Wolves manager, saying: "Major Buckley did not lack a sense of what made headlines. Whether or not monkeys came into the picture I do not know. The injections, which were something quite new in football, were nothing more potent than an immunisation against the common cold, and certainly I do not think they ever helped or hindered me."

Another factor in the improvement in Wolves' League position, at least according to harassed opponents, was their over-zealous tackling. At the end of the 1936-37 season the club was banned by the FA from travelling on a summer tour of the continent as a punishment for receiving too many bookings from referees during the First Division campaign. Many of the cautions had been for arguing with officials, but the FA decision also made it clear they felt that the manager, Buckley, had been personally encouraging unethical football.

The response of the puritanical captain, Cullis, might have cost him his international career. He and the Wolves players felt the slur on Buckley's character was unjustified, and, as skipper, Stan drafted a letter to the FA which all his team-mates signed. It was an action taken without the knowledge of the club, an action inspired by his passionate desire for justice to be seen to be done; he wanted the truth to be told. The letter read: "We should like to state that, far from advocating the rough play we are accused of, Major Buckley is constantly reminding us of the importance of playing good, clean and honest football, and we, as a team, consider you have been most unjust in administering this caution to our manager." This was an era when players and managers were supposed to know their place, when the word of the FA was all-powerful and not to be lightly opposed. Cullis would have known that sending the critical letter might jeopardise the England call-up he craved. He did it anyway.

Again, his moral courage was rewarded, but only after his rival for the international centre-half role, Alf Young of Huddersfield, had been forced to withdraw through injury. On 22 September 1937, still only twenty, Cullis was selected for the Football League team to play the Scottish League at Ibrox. Stanley Matthews was also in the side, but they lost 1-0. When Young failed to recover quickly, his place in the England team for a friendly against Ireland in October 1937 also went to the young centre-half from Wolves. Cullis had still not reached his 21st birthday, and he excelled in a 5-1 victory against the Irish at Windsor Park in Belfast. Chelsea centre-forward George Mills, also making his debut, scored a hat-trick, while Cullis dominated an opponent he was familiar with. "It was an odd coincidence," he recalled, "that I found myself up against Dave 'Boy' Martin, the centre-forward I had faced in the practice match which altered my whole career at Molineux." By that time Martin had left Wolves for Nottingham Forest.

A month later Stan won his second cap in a 2-1 victory against a strong Welsh team in a game played at Ayresome Park, Middlesbrough. That was followed by a 5-4 victory against Czechoslovakia at White Hart Lane in which Stanley Matthews scored a hat-trick. After international matches in London, whether at Wembley or a club ground, Cullis would have to travel back to his West End hotel on the underground train. There were no official FA cars to take players home in those days, so Stan queued up with the fans at the tube station after the match. "If you had a bad game the crowds would instantly recognise you and give you a lot of stick," he told his son years later. It was a powerful incentive to perform well and win the game.

For Cullis these were heady days. Wolves fought a long duel with Arsenal through the spring of 1938 for the League Championship crown. The title was only decided on the final day of the season, when Wolves needed a victory at Roker Park, Sunderland. They lost 1-0 and Arsenal secured the First Division trophy by a single point. It was far from the last time that Stan Cullis would be deprived of winning the Football League title on the last day, both as player and manager.

At least there was the consolation of a place on the England summer tour of Europe. First stop was Berlin, where he was left out of the team in favour of Alf Young. This was the infamous match where the players were ordered by FA officials and England diplomats to give the Heil Hitler salute to a 115,000 crowd which included Nazi leaders Rudolf Hess, Josef Goebbels and Hermann Goering. Cullis was among the England players who, in the dressing-room before the game, had made it clear they were vehemently opposed to the salute being given, diplomacy or no diplomacy. The footballers did not support appeasement. "I remember my father telling me about that day," said his son, the Revd Andrew Cullis. "He was quite opposed to it and protested strongly, as did other players like the captain Eddie Hapgood. It was a three-line whip and the players were forced to do it against their will." Andrew is among many friends and family of Cullis who believed Stan had been in the team that day. In fact he was involved only behind the scenes, where the moral outrage was shared by all. Another England player, Stanley Matthews, recalled: "The dressing-room erupted at the idea. There was bedlam. All the England players were livid and totally opposed to it, and everyone was shouting at once."

England won the game 6-3 in the Olympic Stadium in Berlin, but the devastating scoreline barely merits a footnote in history beside the anger of the afternoon.

Cullis missed the next match of the tour as well, a 2-1 defeat by Switzerland in Zurich in which England's lacklustre attitude brought severe criticism in the press. That partly accounted for the reinstatement of Cullis to the team for the final fixture against France in Paris, which England won 4-2 thanks to two goals from Ted Drake. It restored prestige to the team because the French were one of the strongest sides in Europe at the time.

England's captain at the time, the distinguished Arsenal full-back Eddie Hapgood, immediately warmed to the youngster from Wolverhampton who would become his successor within a year. He said: "Cullis was an intelligent defensive centre-half who varied his play by attacking when warranted. Stanley had mannerisms that could annoy onlookers, but nothing ruffled him, and he was always looking for an opportunity. Stan was always arguing and theorising, one of many lads who were making soccer a stepping stone to a good job when they retired.

"On one foreign tour we were in Paris and some of his team-mates were chipping Stan about his desire to study foreign languages. He took it well in his typically good-natured way. On one sightseeing trip the chipper-in-chief told Stan to ask a benevolent looking Frenchman for directions to a place of interest. Some of the doubters expected Stan to take out his French-English dictionary and stumble through a few phrases. But, to an admiring audience, Stan launched into fluent French to the manner born."

It was an impressive legacy of his desire for self-improvement at night school back in Ellesmere Port, where French had been a subject he studied with passion; it is another example of why Stan Cullis became such a success in football.

Sadly, the last season before war broke out proved to be the pinnacle of Stan's playing career. He was just 22. What a season it was. Wolves went agonisingly close to doing the League and Cup Double, while Cullis himself ended the year as captain of England. There was also a match at Goodison Park, against the eventual champions Everton, which marked the beginning of the end for his life as a centre-half. He collided with Stan Bentham, the Everton centre-forward, was knocked unconscious and carried off on a stretcher. "It was a complete accident," recalled Cullis, "which would not produce any serious consequences in a million other instances. But I spent seven days in bed recovering from concussion." He thought little of the incident at the time; it was just another hazard of sporting combat, particularly as a centre-half constantly charged with taking on craggy centre-forwards in aerial challenges during a time when football was intensely physical and brutal, far more so than today.

In the mid-1960s when Cullis looked back on his playing career, he made a telling comment. "The 'killers' I recall from pre-war days have disappeared," he said. Cullis, in response to these 'killers', was one of the most uncompromising centre-halves with his muscular Christianity.

There was little time for thought with two trophies to chase. A surging run in the FA Cup took Wolves to victories against Bradford Park Avenue, Leicester, Liverpool, Everton and Grimsby, and a place in the Final at Wembley. The 63,315 attendance for the fifth-round tie at home to Liverpool remains the record crowd for a match at Molineux. Their opponents in the Cup Final were Portsmouth, a team struggling at the foot of the First Division, a fact which made Wolves the overwhelming favourites to succeed. Instead, it was an April afternoon which is remembered as one of the greatest upsets in Cup history.

Many reasons were floated for the defeat, some fanciful, others more feasible. The most popular in Cup mythology is the claim by Portsmouth captain Jimmy Guthrie that his team knew the Wolves players were a bag of nerves when they saw their shaky signatures on an autograph book signed by both sides before the game. The book went into the Wolves dressing-room first, and then into Portsmouth's, where Guthrie supposedly discovered the quivering pens of the hot favourites. Cullis himself said of the claim: "Our signatures were supposed to be spidery, but I suspect this discovery was made after the match. Other critics claimed it was a mistake for our team to remain in Wolverhampton until the morning of the match, finally to travel to Wembley amid considerable pomp and excitement. There are arguments on both sides, but I don't think it was a decisive cause of our defeat." Cullis, rather, attributed the 4-1 disaster to the peril of trying to win two trophies and winning neither.

The shaky signatures account is the most romantic version. If there is a grain of truth here, perhaps it is because Guthrie seized on a couple of odd-looking autographs as a tool to help motivate his underdogs. More likely, simply, is that Wolves suffered from the traditional problem of odds-on favourites – complacency. It didn't help that Portsmouth's vital first goal on the half hour was scored by Bert Barlow, an inside-left who had been sold to them by Major Buckley earlier in the season. Such fateful ironies litter the world of football.

Guthrie himself believed the fact that Wolves had many young players was a factor. He said: "While they had the England captain, Cullis, in their side, they also had a few youngsters who would sweat a bit during the preliminaries. Most of our blokes had been around for a few seasons. Cullis and company knew all about us having beaten us 5-0 at Molineux the previous season. But we also knew that Wolves would be playing on an unfamiliar surface. Before there were regulations about the watering of pitches Molineux was a quagmire, and the conditions must have been worth a goal start to Wolves. The Wembley ground was firm and well grassed."

Earlier in the season there had been a particularly special day for Cullis when he played for England against Ireland at Manchester. Alongside him at left-half, making his international debut, was his childhood pal from the back streets of Ellesmere Port, Joe Mercer. Also making his debut was Wolves team-mate William Morris. England won the game 7-0. In April 1939 the trio teamed up again for a 2-1 victory against Scotland in Glasgow, where Bill Shankly was among the opponents. Cullis had been rested from the Wolves team three days before that game on the request of the FA. He watched the League match against Aston Villa from the vantage point of the press box at the back of the main stand at Villa Park. Stan kicked every ball as if he were out on the pitch, leaving the soccer reporters at his side black and blue with bruises. Many who sat next to him on the manager's bench in dug-outs around the world in future years came to know what a painful place it could be.

Success in the League eluded Wolves too. Despite another marvellous campaign they finished second in the First Division table, four points adrift of the champions Everton. For Cullis it was scant consolation that no club had ever before 'won' the runners-up double. The disappointment only fuelled the passion and fury which became the trademark of his managerial style. The many near-miss heartbreaks of his playing career surely help to explain why the centre-half who loved showing off his fancy-dan footwork and artistry became a pragmatic manager who would not tolerate such self-indulgent moments from his own team.

Now, in May 1939, war in Europe looked certain. Appeasement had ended, and the only question was when hostilities would be declared, not how they could be avoided. Cullis signed up for the Territorial Army. When Major Buckley said he would "be very pleased for any of my players who so desire to join the Territorials", Cullis was the first man to do so. He was attached to a battalion of the South Staffordshire Regiment. The question for the England football team was whether their planned summer tour of three European countries – Italy, Yugoslavia and Romania – would go ahead or not? At one stage the Foreign Office was minded to cancel the trip, but eventually it took place, and Cullis became the youngest captain of England.

He regarded this as his finest hour as a player. Looking back, he said: "Representing England was the highlight of my playing career. I've always considered playing for your country to be the highest accolade you can receive."

In his private collection, still in almost mint condition, adorned with a blue ribbon on the front, is the official players' itinerary of the Continental Tour. It makes fascinating reading today in the age of the internet and easy access air travel. At the foot of seventeen days of travel arrangements were the following notes:

(i) Members of the Committee will probably require their Dinner dress.
(ii) The Players will be provided with shirts, knickers and stockings.
(iii) A supply of toilet soap should be taken.

The players boarded the Dover train from Victoria station in London on 9 May and then transferred to the Simplon-Orient Express Train de luxe via Paris on the other side of the channel after crossing to France by steamer. They each had berths in a sleeping car overnight, arriving in Milan at two o'clock in the afternoon to be greeted by such huge crowds that it took them half an hour to make the two-minute walk from the railway station to their hotel. The next day England drew 2-2 against Italy on a muddy, treacle-like pitch at the San Siro stadium, with Stan Matthews, Lawton and Mercer also among the side. A 70,000 crowd was watching behind high fencing put up in case the fans decided to throw missiles at the England players. Italy had won the World Cups of 1934 and 1938 and were the most feared team on the continent. With five minutes left Italy were 2-1 up, and Cullis was sent forward to help the attack along with the other half-backs Mercer and Charlie Willingham. It brought an equaliser when Willie Hall lashed in a goal after England pressure.

A day's rest was followed by another ride on the Orient Express, for an overnight stop at the Grand Hotel in Venice. The next morning it was on the train again to Belgrade, where England faced Yugoslavia at the long-forgotten B.S.K-a stadium. The score was a 2-1 defeat, a result Cullis would later avenge during the war. Now the mode of travel changed. At 11pm the next night the players left Belgrade on a river steamer to sail up the Danube towards Romania. Cabins were reserved and they arrived at Turn-Severin at noon the following day. Here there was a transfer to a train bound for Bucharest, deep in the heart of a Europe anxiously waiting before conflict broke out.

Eddie Hapgood, the classical left-back from Arsenal, was England's established captain at this time. But he had suffered torn ankle ligaments against the rugged Yugoslavs and could not recover in time for the final match of the tour against the Romanians. England needed a new skipper, and the FA delegation, headed by secretary Stanley Rous, later to become head of FIFA, decided on Cullis, the highly impressive captain of Wolves. He was young, but he was a natural leader of men at a time when that quality would shortly be in great demand. Cullis has kept rare photographs of that summer day on Wednesday, 24 May 1939 when he proudly led the team out on to the field at the ground of l'Academie Nationale d'Education Physique in Bucharest. He looked a proud and serious young man in his white England shirt as he handed over a bouquet of flowers to his Romanian counterpart.

The match itself was one-sided thanks to a workmanlike but uninspired England display. The goals were scored by Len Goulden of West Ham and Don Welsh of Charlton during an ill-tempered encounter. The choice of Cullis as captain was fully justified by events as the young skipper forcefully ensured the England team maintained their discipline in the face of severe provocation. Even the normally placid Mercer, the boyhood pal of Cullis, needed his passions reining in that day. Cullis recalled: "One of the Romanians took off the sole of Joe's boot, and I saw Joe threatening him, so I had to tell him, 'If you do anything, I'll send you off, never mind the referee! We're going to finish with eleven men – and win'." So they did, by a 2-0 margin.

For Cullis it was the fulfilment of the fierce ambition Wolves manager Major Buckley had noted in the novice teenager arriving at Molineux from Ellesmere Port only five years earlier.

There has rarely been a swifter ascent to playing glory. Nor a swifter end.

"What I hoped might be the beginning turned out in fact to be the end," recalled Cullis. "The match in Bucharest brought me my twelfth and last official cap for England."

After the game the England squad were taken to Pelash Castle, the home of King Carol of Romania. They were amazed to discover the gardener was a man from London who had answered an advert in the *Evening Standard*. Then Cullis and the players departed on the Arlberg Orient Express via Vienna and Basle. It was a 24-hour train journey across a continent mentally preparing itself for the inevitable conflict that was coming. The players had sensed that wherever they went, particularly on the streets of Milan where they had encountered marchers chanting in support of the Italian dictator Benito Mussolini.

As they ate lunch on the steamer chugging across the Channel from Boulogne to Folkestone none, including the intelligent Cullis, was in any doubt that war would soon be declared. It would change all their lives.

Chapter Four

Company Sergeant Major

"...Often we played matches only a few miles behind the front lines, with the noise of gunfire drowning out the sound of the referee's whistle..." Sir Matt Busby

THE military career of Stan Cullis began in curious fashion. Along with many other patriotic footballers he felt a compelling duty to join the armed forces when war was declared on 3 September 1939. The day before Wolves had lost 2-1 to Blackpool in the third match of the new season, but the League was swiftly abandoned. Cullis was already in the territorials, but now he wanted a full-time role in the army. However, he encountered an immediate and surprising problem. One of the most famous sportsmen in England and Europe failed his medical and was declared unfit for service.

This was one of the favourite stories he would tell to his children and grandchildren in later years. Son Andrew said: "My father has always had a very low pulse, and when he went sign for the army at the start of the war he failed the medical because of that. They told him, 'You can't join up because you're not fit enough'.

"He said to the doctor, 'I'm the captain of the England football team. I can't be unfit'.

"But the bloke wouldn't change his mind and wrote down FAILED on his form. Well, the word went around that the Wolves had fiddled it and got him off, and that really upset my father. So he tried again, and the next doctor knew who he was and had been alerted to the situation. He said: 'fine, first-class fitness' – and didn't even bother examining him. That's how Stan Cullis joined the army."

It seems absurd in retrospect that the football authorities tried to begin the 1939-40 season at all. Many players had already planned to join the forces, and there were delayed kick-offs to matches at Highbury and Craven Cottage because of one-way traffic schemes in surrounding streets designed to help with the first war evacuations of children from London. Yet there was a powerful feeling, too, that normal life had to continue as much as possible, and throughout the war years football matches were encouraged as an entertainment for servicemen and civilians alike. Numbers on shirts to help identify players began at this time.

Professional footballers took many roles in the war effort. Giant goalkeeper Frank Swift, an England team-mate of Cullis, decided on the role of a special constable in Manchester. On his first day of traffic duty he became so confused that he fled his post and left the flow of cars and trucks and buses to itself. "I felt at that moment how many full-backs must have felt when playing against Stanley Matthews." he admitted.

Raich Carter, another England legend, joined the auxiliary fire service, while Albert Stubbins, later to foil Cullis's hopes of Championship winner's medal, became a draughtsman in a Sunderland shipyard. George Mutch, who had scored the dramatic last-minute penalty winner in the 1938 FA Cup Final for Preston North End, worked as a class one riveter, building aeroplanes.

Many of the most famous players, like Joe Mercer, Matt Busby and Cullis himself, were propelled into the Army Physical Training Corp where their sporting talent and the leadership qualities which would later make them renowned First Division managers, could be best utilised. Mercer and Busby were among an early intake of physical training instructors from a scheme devised by the Football Association. They enlisted on the basis of a firm promise that the rank of sergeant instructor would be given them to immediately.

When it didn't happen, when they discovered the stripes were not an automatic award and might need to be earned, there was anger in the dressing-room. Mercer recalled: "When we were told that we were not going to become sergeants right away we mutinied. We refused to obey orders. It was out of ignorance really. Our ignorance let us assume that we should be accepted immediately as sergeant instructors on the same terms as men who had worked for years and undergone specialised courses to win their tapes."

Was Cullis among the men who took that mutinous line? From all the evidence we have of his character at the time, he would have been more dismayed than anyone by the thought of broken promises. But it is also hard to imagine him taking part in any kind of unofficial mutiny. That wasn't his style. Happily, a solution was found as Football Association officials suggested the famous soccer stars be made temporary sergeants. The generals agreed to the compromise, although the regular army sergeants gave the footballers a hard time.

Cullis's official army service book, a battered and tatty relic of six and a half years in uniform, provides confirmation that he was promoted to the rank of acting sergeant on 27 November 1939. It was a rank fully confirmed only the following year on 27 October 1940, two days after his 24th birthday. The dates fit in with Mercer's recollections of confused and uncertain months for all Englishmen.

As with every soldier there are obligatory entries in the Service and Pay Book. His army number was 4917447, and his Trade on Enlistment was entered as: Professional footballer. Religion was written in a firm hand as: C of E. It seems strange, however, that the answers to his place of birth and the nationality of his father and mother have been obliterated with a black crayon mark.

If the services were initially unsure how to deal with the famous footballers in their midst at the start of the conflict, there is no doubt that the game and its benefit to the war effort grew in importance through the years of battle. Many members of the Royal family and countless politicians would travel to watch international matches at Wembley between England and the other home nations. Even Winston Churchill, who had no instinctive love of the working-man's sport, attended fixtures. He was introduced to Cullis among other footballers before an England v Scotland clash in 1941 – along with seven other Cabinet ministers and the King of Greece. Churchill may not have been too aware of the intricacies of the offside law or the W-M tactical formation of the teams, but he understood well enough the propaganda value of sport and the helpful psychological effect on morale of soldiers being trained in fitness by sporting heroes.

One of the proudest letters in Stan Cullis's collection is one from 10 Downing Street on 24 January 1942. It reads:

Dear Sgt Major Cullis,
I am writing to thank you very much indeed for the part you played in making the representative match which took place at Wembley on Saturday, 17 January such an outstanding success. The magnificent donation, which will be received by my "Aid To Russia" Appeal as a result of the match, will enable the Red Cross and St John War Organisation to procure many of those supplies which are so urgently needed in Russia to alleviate the sufferings of her soldiers and civilian population.
Yours very truly,
Clementine Churchill.

Cullis was initially stationed at one of the traditional homes of the British Army in Aldershot. The small town's football team has rarely made any headlines, save for when it was closed down in the early 1990s due to lack of funds. During the war it became one of the most powerful teams in the land, able to field countless international stars because of the guest-player system that operated, including the famous Mercer-Cullis-Britton half-back line which many consider among the finest of all-time. When the matches were strictly for entertainment purposes it really didn't matter which team you played for; all previous club contracts had been suspended when war broke out.

There were also numerous wartime internationals and army matches. An early such example was a British Army v French Army match in Paris during the so-called Phoney War before Germany invaded Western European nations in the summer of 1940. Tommy Lawton remembered the journey across the Channel for the game.

"We took the train down to Dover," recalled Lawton, "and Stan Cullis told us he had acquired some new pills that were guaranteed to prevent sea-sickness. They would only cost one guinea, and Matt Busby and I thought that would be a guinea well spent. Once on the ship we went downstairs, took our pills and began to play cards. Everything went well and after a couple of hours Stan was very pleased and thought we must be nearing France. Someone overheard this and pointed out there had been a delay and we hadn't even left Dover yet. When we did leave port the three of us dead-heated for the side of the ship and were very ill. I spent the entire journey on deck in the cold and caught the flu."

The incident was typical Stan Cullis, a man always in search of the new, always eager to experiment and test out new theories and products.

Even if wartime football was essentially an entertainment, the instinctive will-to-win did not desert talented and committed footballers. Stan Mortensen, the Blackpool and England centre-forward, recalled a match against Cullis during the war in Bruges. He said: "One of the newspaper cuttings I cherished was about 'Cullis's bad day'. The British Army team were playing the paratroop red devils towards the end of the war. Stan, always the idealist, was trying to keep the ball in play and tried to nod ball down to his his own feet. I was able to nip in and take the ball away and score before he could recover."

Aldershot were keen to capitalise on their new status to triumph in some of the war trophies, and so were other clubs. Some maestros became mercenaries. Scottish international Bill Shankly, a Cup Final winner with Preston in 1938 and later the celebrated manager of Liverpool, remembered his experience, saying: "People found me. They came looking for the players who had reached international standing. It was easy to be found, even in the big camps, where there were maybe thousands of men. Word soon got around. I played for many teams and had a game every Saturday." According to Shankly, the desire to play was not just about extra cash, but also a desire to maintain match fitness. Many footballers could not play as regularly as they wanted or needed to. It was often the case, too, that players would turn out under assumed names because they were actually absent without leave from their camps or barracks.

There were four clubs for which Cullis played during this ad-hoc time. Over five years he appeared 38 times for Aldershot, 29 for Wolves, eighteen for Fulham and eight for Liverpool. Wolves won the North Cup in 1942, but Cullis did not play in the 6-3 victory against Sunderland in the Final. His place was filled by a youth team rookie called Billy Wright. Added to this were twenty wartime internationals for England and various other matches for the English or British Army XI at home or abroad.

It might have been more but for the broken ankle he sustained during a tempestuous match between Fulham and Portsmouth on 21 March 1942. Cullis was outraged, both by the tackle, which left him severely injured, and by the roughhouse attitude of the opposition players. He was convinced the injury had been deliberately caused and wrote to the Football Association complaining bitterly about events. The puritan streak in his character was on show again. The FA's War Emergency Committee met to discuss the angry Cullis letter, and delivered the following verdict.

"Sergeant Instructor Cullis acted rightly in bringing to the notice of the Football Association the circumstances of his injury, and we agree that the relations between certain players of the two teams were hostile and that the match started in a bad spirit. But there was insufficient evidence to prove that Cullis's injury was deliberately caused.

"To Referees we issue the following instruction – that War conditions are not to be made the excuse for laxity in the execution of their duties."

By this time Cullis had been married, to Winifred Weldon, a girl brought up in the quiet, privileged villages on the Berkshire-Surrey borders close to Aldershot. Her world was very different to his own, but one he aspired to. She recalled their courtship to Geoffrey Green, football correspondent of *The Times*, saying: "Stan and I met during the War. He was in the army and we walked out for some time before we got married. Not once did he say what he had done before in civvy street. It was only later, after we had wed, that I discovered he was a footballer – and the captain of England!"

We may view this as another example of the secrets Cullis kept throughout his life, or perhaps as an illustration of how his puritan nature meant he would not trade on his sporting status for the sake of romance.

His son Andrew has a simpler answer, explaining: "What happened was that my mother came from Berkshire and there was a swimming pool called the Pantiles in the Virginia Water area. She couldn't really swim but she went there because the army dropped in for a swim and that's where all the girls went. She met my father at the pool. He must have said he played some football and she told her father about this.

"Her father then became terribly cross because he assumed it was village football and was all for stopping the budding romance. So I think my father stopped mentioning anything about football because of that. They were pretty keen on each other."

Winifred and Stan were married on 5 July 1941 at Sunningdale in Berkshire – at a time when Cullis was probably at the peak of his powers as a professional footballer.

Certainly, he was a first choice selection for every England international. Soccer writer Frank Butler was asked by the *Sunday Express* that year to name his six most valuable footballers to the national side. He put Stan Cullis at the top of the list, just ahead of Stanley Matthews and Tommy Lawton. Matthews himself remembered a match played in freezing weather, against Scotland in January 1942 at Wembley, which England won 3-0 with two goals from centre-forward Lawton. He recalled: "Cullis was outstanding in the centre of defence that day. He used to be one of my motivations during training routines. When I worked on my skills and speed it was to keep one step ahead; the thought of being on the end of a crunching tackle from Stan Cullis focused my mind totally."

England v Scotland encounters during the war stirred the blood just as surely as during peace time. Often the half-back collisions would feature Cullis and Mercer in the white English jerseys against Shankly and Busby in the blue Scottish shirts. The Scots rarely won – even when England had to borrow one of their opponents because only ten players had turned up at Hampden due to travel difficulties.

Cullis's most vivid recollection was of a 4-0 victory in Glasgow in April 1943. The crowd had been officially restricted to 75,000 due to emergency regulations, but fans stormed into Hampden and an estimated 105,000 saw the game in which England's captain, Cullis, suffered a nasty injury when grabbed in a tender area of his anatomy by the Scottish forward Dougie Wallace, at a free-kick. A brawl developed and Cullis later recalled the incident with amusement, saying: "I floppin ran all over the pitch for the last ten minutes trying to kick him – but I couldn't catch him."

Poor Wallace never played for his country again as punishment. Was that due, perhaps, to the reputation and influence Cullis had now acquired?

He would also tell his Wolves players in later years, when they were moaning about conditions, of his journey to and from that match. Bill Slater, who played for England in the 1958 World Cup, said: "He always told us about the story about going to Glasgow and back in war standing all the way on the train on the both the journey up to Scotland and the one coming home!"

Later in 1943 came what Cullis called "the finest football I have ever seen." It was played by England against Scotland at Maine Road, Manchester as they won the match 8-0. Joe Mercer reckoned it was "the greatest game I can remember," while Stanley Matthews thought it "the most memorable wartime international, a day when England were irresistible." Another man in the team was renowned cricketer-footballer Denis Compton. Tommy Lawton scored four goals.

Another international against Wales brought criticism for captain Cullis from the press because Stanley Matthews rarely received the ball on the right wing, a deliberate tactic initiated by the influential skipper. Cullis recalled it many years later, saying: "As captain I had quite a big say in strategy then because there was no manager – just selectors. I heard before the game that Wales were going to put two men on Stanley Matthews. As a result, I decided we would attack on the left through Denis Compton instead of on the right through Stan. We won handsomely but the newspapers gave me a right rollicking and asked how I'd dared treat Stanley Matthews like that. They insisted the spectators had gone to watch Matthews, not me, and demanded that I be forced to give up the captaincy. Then I had a letter from Stanley Rous at the FA which said: 'You will remain as captain.' It was nice to know I had the backing of the people who really mattered."

None of these games counted as official caps, but there seems little doubt the quality of play was at times outstanding. Whatever the difficulties, whatever the pain of conflict, the show went on. When Singapore fell to the Japanese there was a significant loss of rubber-supply, which meant fewer of the bladders inside the footballs of the day could be manufactured. Production was cut by three-quarters, and, to compensate, balls would be used for many matches rather than the usual one. Player movement was also a problem. Trains might be cancelled at short notice or roads closed. Cullis and his colleagues did the best they could.

Back among the clubs, business also continued. So did the endless politicking that goes on behind the scenes at all grounds. In February 1944 Cullis received a letter from an influential figure in Wolverhampton football, John Ireland, typed on headed notepaper from his second-hand car dealership in the town. It read:

> "I enclose for your very special attention a copy of the Express & Star in which you will note that Major Buckley is making very determined efforts to leave the Wolves. Forgive me if I appear too much of a nosey parker, but this is a big subject in Wolverhampton and I have talked to many people concerning it and your name has been spoken of on quite a few occasions as Buckley's successor. It would cause no surprise in Wolverhampton. I trust that you are keeping well, my respects to your wife."

Here is the first recorded hint of Stan Cullis becoming manager of the Wolves. Buckley was about to quit for "personal reasons" and moved on to Notts County. It was impossible at the time, of course, for Sergeant Instructor Cullis, aged 27, to become the boss at Molineux, and the job was taken by former Welsh international winger Ted Vizard, who joined from Queen's Park Rangers. He was chosen from more than 100 applicants for the post.

Ireland's letter is deeply ironic. Twenty years later, when the second-hand car salesman had become chairman of Wolves, he was the man who callously sacked the Iron Manager.

The leadership qualities of Cullis blossomed during the war. Where some footballers like Stanley Matthews instinctively recoiled from giving commands, the need for strong men to inspire others won recognition in the services. "Army football people still hold him in high regard," revealed his son Andrew. "My father used to train the commandos, and I remember him talking about these really tough blokes. He would tell me how he used to go up with them in the aeroplane on their first parachute jumps – and how they were all in a quiet, dark corner saying a prayer. 'They weren't quite so tough then', he would say.

"My father organised many of the internationals played in the war and it was a time when he developed the attributes that had already made him a very young captain of Wolves and England. It was in the army that he developed the sternness which became his enduring public image."

Joe Mercer took over as England skipper during the war when Cullis was unavailable, and was as proud as his old friend. He said: "Captaincy must be spontaneous. Players who want to take this responsibility are not common and I think good captains are born to the job. I am sure Stan Cullis was."

Cullis's final three England appearances came in the first few months of 1944. There were two more victories against the Scots, and then a 2-0 triumph against Wales at Ninian Park in May. In both the Scotland games he was opposed by Matt Busby, and although they were fierce rivals then and later as managers, it was also the beginning of a lifelong friendship that meant more to Cullis than almost any other.

They should have been team-mates at Aldershot when both were available to play for the club. But it was felt wrong that the captains of both England and Scotland should guest for one team, so Busby graciously stood down.

Life changed dramatically when the army gave Cullis a serious promotion in July 1944. He became a Company Sergeant Major and was posted to Bari on the Adriatic coast after the successful Allied invasion of Italy. Busby was there too, and the pair talked incessantly about football. It is not far-fetched to believe that this unlikely setting was where the two greatest managers of the 1950s began to plot their football ideas and tactics and success.

Cullis's son said: "The friendship with Busby developed in the war and the bond between them was very strong. To me he was Uncle Matt. I don't think there was anyone else in football who was my 'uncle'. That's how close they were. I can remember coming home on the day of the Munich air crash and being told that 'Uncle Matt' had been involved in the disaster. They were so close, and although they decided on very different styles of play for their clubs I am sure many of their ideas on management were forged in those long conversations."

One of the reasons for the posting was to make Cullis a football manager for the first time. He recalled: "Not long after I arrived in Bari my colonel summoned me and ordered me to find a British team which could defeat the Yugoslavian Partizan army team which had been wiping the floor with services' sides throughout the Mediterranean area. So keen was the army to redeem its football prestige that I was allowed to pick my team from the whole of the Central Mediterranean Forces." What a wealth of talent he had at his disposal. There was Bryn Jones, a former Wolves team-mate who had been transferred to Arsenal before the war for a then world record £14,000 sum. And there was a young lad from Preston whose potential Cullis had instantly recognised. He was Tom Finney.

The Partizan invincibles were thrashed 7-2 in front of a 45,000 crowd. Jones netted a hat-trick, while Cullis played superbly himself at centre-half. It was his first taste of putting the pride back into English football – but certainly not the last. Photographs he has kept from that scorching afternoon reveal a packed stadium in Bari, the supporters of both teams waving flags and banners; the atmosphere apparently frenzied. British troops from every part of southern Italy had been allowed to attend the game, some travelling through the night on lorries or trains.

In the middle of it all Cullis looks impeccably calm and controlled. He remembered later his only worry had been when Yugoslav women fighters from the Partizans came into the office he had been given, casually wearing hand grenades on their belts. He didn't think that was proper for ladies.

After the match he wrote a letter to Frank Butler of the Express; it was one of the ways sporting news from abroad reached the public. The newspaper published Cullis's view that: "In my opinion young Tom Finney is the best discovery of the war, and in my opinion he is the successor to Stanley Matthews."

Butler added his own observation, saying: "That is high praise from Cullis, who is most reserved in his judgements."

There were many other such football matches organised. The Polish Corps XI were beaten 10-2. In the back of his soldier's service and pay book, Cullis scribbled down teams and phone numbers galore. It must have been quite a feat of logistics to gather together a strong side from camps across the whole of southern Europe when the ferocity of war was so close at hand. Photographs show that he often didn't play in these games, instead directing them from the touchline while wearing his army uniform, combat shorts and all. There is no doubt looking at them who is in charge of proceedings.

Matt Busby played in that army touring side as often as he could, and retained a lasting memory of how adjacent to the battle-field they would play their matches, saying: "Often we played only a few miles behind the front lines, with the noise of gunfire sometimes tending to drown the sound of the referee's whistle." It was much appreciated by their superiors. A commanding officer on the Italian front told Cullis that one football exhibition game was worth five entertainment shows to the morale of the troops.

Just before Cullis left Bari he suffered another serious concussion injury. He was confined to bed in a military hospital for five days after being knocked unconscious during a low-key unit match. He was beginning to realise that his playing days could not last too much longer. A year earlier, 1943, an even more severe incident had happened. Ironically it was on the same Goodison Park ground where his initial problem had occurred back in 1938 when he had collided with the Everton forward Stan Bentham. Almost on the same spot on the pitch, Cullis was again knocked out when a fierce shot caught him full on the chin playing in a match between the British Army and the Scottish Army.

"Again I was carried off the Goodison field, with even more serious consequences," recalled Cullis. "I was on the danger list in a Liverpool hospital for five days, and altogether on my back for nearly a fortnight. I resolved that a repetition of these incidents could only have one ending – complete retirement from football."

It seems remarkable now that a footballer could be on the 'danger list' simply for being struck by a ball. But the balls then were so different, becoming incredibly heavy on wet days as water soaked into them. Even the laces which closed the leather over the inside bladders could be a problem. Gilbert Allsop, the centre-forward who scored both Walsall's goals in a famous giant-killing FA Cup victory against Arsenal in 1933, had his career ended when a loose lace blinded him in one eye.

Cullis's son Andrew wonders whether constant heading of those balls had a detrimental effect on his father's health, not only then, but also later in life. He said: "I think all those times he had severe concussions probably contribute to his memory loss now. Perhaps the most likely reason is the pounding my father's head took playing the game when he did. Very often the ball was not only heavy, but also covered with ice when they played on frozen pitches. He did a lot of heading and he didn't have much hair! He wondered about that himself in later years when he suffered a couple of strokes."

As the Allies began to close in on victory towards the end of the war in late 1944, so the minds of everyone, including former professional footballers, started to focus on what would happen back in civvy street. Many players had lost their lives, others like Cullis had merely given up the best years of their sporting careers, and he knew that was a small price, saying: "Not for one moment did I bemoan what I might have lost, like more England caps. I came home from the war in one piece and that was something to be grateful for. We all know that a lot of young men were not so lucky."

For those who survived and were still of playing age the two main questions were whether they would go back to the club which had held their registration five years earlier, and how much they would be paid in the brave new post-war world?

Cullis was deeply aware of the issue, and because of his position as England captain and then 'manager' of army touring sides, he knew that his thoughts might carry more weight than most. He wrote another of his letters to the newspapers back home in November 1944, this time to the *Daily Sketch*, which dubbed him 'the most influential professional footballer in the country'.

He wanted to fight for the rights of his fellow players, just as he had for his own contract as a teenager and then for the reputation of Wolves manager Major Buckley in 1937. Company Sergeant Major Cullis's letter read:

"During my recent football tour of the Fifth and Eighth Army fronts I had the opportunity of discussing with many professional players the proposed post-war plans of the League players. The players have awaited these plans with eager expectancy, confident that many of the pre-war anomalies would be adjusted. The reported proposals have brought disillusionment and the realisation that the plans are nothing except an obvious attempt to protect the clubs at the expense of the players. Four pounds per week! Do the League planners imagine they can foist any system on to the long-suffering players? While the proposed £4 a week may be perfectly agreeable to the professionals who miraculously became skilled workers overnight at the outbreak of war, and who will presumably carry on at the steady jobs during the transitional period, the lot of the professional who has served five years in the Services and who will have to pick up the threads he left off becomes, to say the least, an unenviable one. To the fathers of boys contemplating launching their sons into the uncertain seas of professional football I would say: 'Think, and just go on thinking.'"

It is the message of a passionate trade union shop steward arguing for better wages and working conditions. In November 1943 the players' union had proposed the abolition of the maximum wage and greatly increased bonus payments for important matches like FA Cup semi-finals and Finals. They also wanted revised conditions for transfers, player representation on committees and a minimum £4 a week salary if the maximum wage could not be abolished.

At the end of the conflict the people of Britain voted in a new Labour government at the expense of inspirational war leader Winston Churchill. Many new schemes to benefit the working class man like the National Health Service were instituted. Footballers mostly failed in their militancy, even though they voted in favour of a nationwide strike in November 1945. The maximum wage stayed, although some concessions like the £4 a week minimum pay were made by the conservative football authorities.

Cullis had two particular personal worries when he returned home from Italy in December 1945 on leave pending demobilisation. One was simply about being fit enough for the resumption of League soccer. "Could I pick up threads of football life?" he wondered. "Largely because of the conditions in Italy, where the heat was intense, my normal fighting weight of 12st 7lbs had gone down to 11st 4lbs. For a long time, too, like many of my colleagues, I had lived on tins of army food as we travelled the dusty roads of Italy in lorries to keep football appointments."

The second was which club he should play for. Mrs Cullis had a good job based in London, and her husband's initial desire was to be granted a transfer from Wolves and play his remaining seasons in the capital. There was talk of interest from both Arsenal and Chelsea, but they baulked at the £20,000 transfer fee being discussed in the newspaper columns. The other factor was Wolves' determination to hang on to their England captain. As the national players' dispute over terms and conditions had shown, the clubs were still all-powerful. Cullis remained at Wolves, but no doubt with his position and standing within Molineux further enhanced.

He hardly played for Wolves in the interim 1945-46 season, in which there was no official League championship and the FA Cup was played on a two-leg basis. Cullis had one final army posting abroad, to Frederikstad in Norway for a week in the middle of May 1946. He also did soccer coaching there with the local club. The Norwegian pass he was issued with, stamped by officials, is among his documents. In his book *All For The Wolves* Cullis said that he was selected on 'sentimental' grounds for one final England match, a Victory International against France played in Paris that same week, but that he had to withdraw after suffering a leg injury. The two facts don't tally.

Was Cullis's a diplomatic version of events? Could it have been that the imposition of one last military duty forced him to miss a final England match, and that he responded to the disappointment with silent honour? Or was the unlikely posting to

Norway a way of helping Cullis to get away from it all? We shall never know. It is another of the secrets of the Iron Manager's life.

By now it was no secret he would become a football boss. But even before Cullis had left Italy, Matt Busby had been named the new manager of Manchester United in October 1945. He had beaten his great friend to the punch; but not by long – and the pair would soon enough be trading blows throughout the golden years of 1950s English club football.

Chapter Five

The Last Season

"...I didn't want to go down in history as the man who decided the destiny of a championship with a professional foul..." Stan Cullis

HOW different the history of football might have been had Stan Cullis accepted his first lucrative offer to become a manager in the summer of 1946. It was made by ambitious Third Division North club Hull City on the recommendation of Cullis's mentor at Wolves in the 1930s, Major Frank Buckley. The approach was not an easy one to resist; the salary easily outstripped the maximum wage he could be paid as a player, and a luxury house was thrown in too as part of the deal by the Hull chairman, Harold Needler, who was in the process of building a fine new stadium called Boothferry Park.

Cullis met Needler for detailed talks and was on the brink of departing Molineux. Through the war it had become obvious to anyone with an eye for football that the Wolves captain was management material, and the series of concussion injuries he had suffered had already made him wary of playing for too much longer, even though he was only 29-years-old and still very much a candidate for the England national team.

He recalled: "I was very tempted to accept the post, In fact, my mind was made up. First I spoke to Mr Joe Baker, the chairman of Wolves, to tell him that I was retiring and that the club would need a new centre-half for the 1946-47 season. He asked me to speak to the directors and they persuaded me to stay."

Three factors influenced that difficult decision for Cullis. One was the promise by the Wolves board that he would become assistant manager at Molineux to Ted Vizard the moment he eventually retired as a player. The second was a desire to win a League Championship title or FA Cup Cup winners' medal which had so narrowly eluded him and the club in the two seasons before war broke out. Cullis sensed that Wolves still had a wonderful team, especially with sparkling talents like goalkeeper Bert Williams, the magnificent Billy Wright, sprightly Jesse Pye and wingers Johnny Hancocks and Jimmy Mullen in the side. The third was simply loyal affection for Wolverhampton Wanderers, the club he had always been destined to serve.

He decided he could afford to wait at least one more season before following Matt Busby into a manager's office.

So, on 31 August 1946, almost seven years to the day after Football League soccer had been abandoned to fight a world war, the old gold shirts of Wolves were led out on to the field again for a proper match by skipper Stan Cullis. The jutting forehead was even more pronounced now that he was almost completely bald, the tackles were as crunching as ever, his arms and elbows still worked like pistons to deter opposition players. Perhaps he wasn't quite as quick off the mark as he used to be, but that hardly seemed to matter on a Saturday afternoon when Wolves overwhelmed the visitors, Arsenal, by a 6-1 scoreline in front of an ecstatic 50,845 crowd. What a way to start, and what a vindication for Cullis.

Then, of the next five matches, one was drawn and four were lost, surely due to complacency and over-confidence after the thrashing of Arsenal. The team recovered its composure, winning twelve of the subsequent fifteen games to lead the First Division table by the first week of December. This was obviously going to be no ordinary season as massive crowds all round the country watched the return of competitive football action. Prices of just over one shilling per game bought tickets to the best show in town, entertainment rivalled only by film stars like Humphrey Bogart on the big cinema screens.

The plot for Cullis's final days as a player was hardly more believable than some of those dreamed up in Hollywood.

His fear of suffering another head injury came true in the depths of winter. In a match away to Middlesbrough the ball became covered in ice on a frozen pitch, and the Wolves captain was constantly heading it away to thwart attacks by the home side. He collapsed on the train home after the game and was taken to a hospital in Sheffield, the next stop on the line. "I spent a week there," recalled Cullis. "I was examined by a specialist who had recently been consulted by Bruce Woodcock, the British heavyweight boxing champion, and this doctor confirmed my fears when he said that I should retire at once. I was only thirty, and the thought wasn't a happy one. After considerable thought I decided to compromise and finish the season."

It was a decision Cullis took in almost total secrecy. None of his team-mates were aware of either the calculated gamble he was taking with his long-term health, nor the fact that he would retire come what may when the 1946-47 campaign ended. To tell them, he reasoned, would be unfair; it might compromise the way they played in relation to him, perhaps going for headers that should be his as a centre-half. It was also typical of his nature to keep any problems in his life firmly kept from public view, the lid to the bottle of his swirling private thoughts tightly shut.

Why did he risk his health? The pursuit of glory is the only answer, allied, maybe, to a sense of loyalty to many, if not quite all, of his team-mates.

Frost and snow, ice and rain; the freakishly arctic winter cruelly interrupted the flow of Wolves' season. Many of their matches in early 1947 were cancelled due to the bad weather, and the Government refused to sanction midweek fixtures to catch up for the lost games citing a 'National Emergency'. In a time of ration books and recovery from war that could hardly be quibbled at. One major problem was the worry that if Wednesday afternoon matches were played (the floodlight era had not begun) it might encourage mass absenteeism of workers wanting to watch their football teams playing important games. That was enough of a problem on normal Saturday afternoons anyway.

Wolves had been made clear favourites to win the FA Cup by the bookmakers, but one element of Cullis's dream to finish with a winners' medal was snuffed out when the side lost in a fourth round replay to Sheffield United. The stop-start nature of their schedule at that time probably contributed to a surprise defeat. At one stage of the winter they did not play a match for five weeks.

By the beginning of March, however, and with a number of matches in hand on their keenest rivals like Liverpool and Stoke, Wolves were top of the First Division table again after exciting wins against Derby 7-2 and Chelsea 6-4. Winning a first-ever Championship for the club was in the players' own hands thanks mainly to the inspired defensive work of Cullis and the endless goalscoring of centre-forward Dennis Westcott. In their first 32 games of the season Wolves conceded only 36 goals, making them far and away the meanest defence in the country. Dr Percy Young, in his history of the club, wrote: "Throughout the season Cullis guided his side with uncanny judgement. The value of his own play is directly reflected in the low tally of goals scored against the team."

In attack the form of Westcott was crucial. On 10 May he broke the club's League individual scoring record when he netted his 37th League goal of the season. A week later he was injured in a match at home to Blackburn and missed the vital last two games of the season.

Superficially, that seemed the most devastating blow to the team's chances of securing the title. They found it fiendishly hard to score in the remaining matches. But, beneath the surface, there were also simmering tensions within the dressing-room which affected the team's performances and meant they had to endure a famous all-or-nothing final match of the season against Liverpool on 31 May when the title should already have been won.

An astonishingly frank letter was written to Cullis on 21 May

1947 by club chairman Joe Baker, who had made his money as a nurseryman and florist in the Black Country. It came on headed notepaper from his Seed and Flower Farm at Codsall, Wolverhampton. It reads:

> "I agree we can't leave the announcement regarding your future much longer, but am of the opinion it would be better left until the question of the Championship is settled. Nothing has been said yet to Mr Vizard, nor would any good purpose be served by discussing the matter with him until the Board have decided on how the management of the Club is to be reorganised.
>
> "We all realise you cannot have proper discipline as long as one or two players are allowed to do more or less as they like, but with the Championship almost in sight it wasn't considered wise to run the risk of showdown during the last few weeks although I admit it might have been unnecessary if the job had been tackled firmly when the trouble started earlier in the season. I know that many things which have happened must have been very galling to yourself, and I think the time has come when it would be advisable to have a clean-up even if it means starting with a weaker and somewhat unsettled side next season."

The letter begs so many questions about Wolverhampton Wanderers on the brink of winning the League title. How could the manager, Ted Vizard, not be aware of Cullis's imminent retirement, nor the Board's promise to make Cullis assistant manager? How much influence did Cullis already have behind the scenes at Molineux? Which players were the troublemakers who should have faced a showdown over their poor attitude? The implication in Baker's message to the club captain is that Cullis had secretly protested to the Board about Vizard's weak management, fearing it would cost the team's chances of success dear. The implication is that Cullis wanted to tell his team-mates and manager about his own personal situation far earlier, instead of waiting until the hotel lunch prior to Wolves' final match against Liverpool. And the implication is that the announcement was delayed to suit the convenience of a machinating Board of Directors.

What is obvious, too, is Cullis's private fury and disdain for self-centred team-mates and players who were allegedly poisoning the atmosphere in the Molineux dressing-room. Was this one of the crucial lessons he learned in developing his philosophy and practice of management? Certainly, the Iron Manager did not tolerate prima donna characters when he took charge of the club.

Many of the answers to these questions will never be known. But the picture painted by Baker's extraordinary letter is not a happy one, and it perhaps explains, for the first time, the profoundest reason why Wolves threw away what had seemed for many months to be the certainty of becoming League champions.

Still to come was the greatest drama of Stan Cullis's playing career – his last fateful match at Molineux, the title decider against Liverpool.

The sum was simple for the home side. If Wolves won the match they were guaranteed to be champions. No-one could overtake them at the top. If Liverpool were winners, they could also be champions, but would have to wait for the result of Stoke City's last match to be played a few days later.

Optimism was high among club supporters totally unaware of the shenanigans going on behind the scenes at Molineux. The evening football paper was printed on ceremonial gold paper rather than the usual pink of the Saturday sports edition. It was all ready for sale apart from a space left for the match report.

I make no apologies for retracing the story outlined in the opening chapter. I do so because it illustrates most clearly the character of Stan Cullis as a man and as a footballer.

His secret retirement plan was finally revealed to stunned Wolves colleagues at the team lunch at a hotel in Sutton Coldfield. "This is a wonderful club," he told them. "I want to thank you all from the bottom of my heart for the many ways in which you have helped me." Billy Wright, who would succeed Cullis as captain, remembered only the rising emotion of the occasion, the huge desire among the players to win the game for their respected skipper. "Stan's voice was choked with emotion and there were tears in his eyes," said Wright.

The Molineux crowd were equally stunned by the news as Cullis took to the pitch before the game to publicly announce his departure as a player. He spoke about his desire to leave with a winners' medal and recalled the savage disappointment of the 1939 Cup Final against Portsmouth. The Liverpool players preparing in their dressing-room, at least according to Albert Stubbins, knew nothing of this addition to the fever pitch atmosphere of a 50,000 crowd. "We could hear the noise, of course," recalled Stubbins. "But you would have expected that for such a tense and important match. We knew how difficult it would be. For myself, I was up against the great Stan Cullis, a magnificent footballer who had been captain of England. You knew you had been tackled by him, and we had some great battles out on the pitch, although it was always played fair and by the rules. In the dressing-room we were concentrating on the match."

Did the shock of hearing Cullis's news affect the Wolves team as they conceded an early goal to Jack Balmer? How can we know more than fifty years later? A showdown for the League title had more than enough tension riding on it anyway.

The crucial moment of the match played in blazing 96-degree heat came midway through the first half. Stubbins, who later became a football journalist, can still picture it with perfect clarity. "We had a move we tried quite often, of chipping the ball over a defence for me to run onto," he said. "Because I knew the pass was coming it gave me a two or three yard start on the centre-half who was my direct opponent. When it worked well the pass would allow me enough time to race clear. This one was perfect. I had the start I needed on Stan. He was still trying to turn while I was running on to the ball and I knew there was no way he could catch me without a foul.

"But all he had to do was pull my jersey and he'd have stopped me in my tracks. I could hear him behind me, but he was too big a man to stoop to that kind of tactic, even though in those days he probably wouldn't even have been booked, never mind sent off. He couldn't bring himself to do it and I really admired him for that."

In the modern era there is little doubt a defender would have fouled Stubbins. Other centre-halves in 1947 would have done so too, a view held by Stubbins himself. But not Stan Cullis. He would not compromise the principles of right and wrong which he had first learned as a young boy at St Thomas's Church in Ellesmere Port. Contemporaries like Stanley Matthews and Tom Finney have gone into soccer legend for their famed gentlemanly attitude and behaviour on the pitch – and there is no doubt that Cullis was their equal, even if history has never given him his proper due for it. He did indeed have iron in his soul.

There was, of course, still plenty of time in the final game of his career for Wolves to try to recover. In the second half they rallied superbly, and new hope was forged when Jimmy Dunn scored a fine goal. But Liverpool goalkeeper Cyril Sidlow, who had played for Wolves in the war and still trained at Molineux through the week, stood firm. The final whistle brought a great sadness to Cullis, as Stubbins testified. "I vividly remember going up to shake his hand at the final whistle and seeing that Stan was crying," said the Liverpool centre-forward. "There were tears in his eyes, and I can assure you he wasn't hamming it up. He wasn't that kind of man. He was a hard footballer, and it was an indication of just how much it had meant to him."

The testimony of men like Stubbins and Billy Wright to witnessing a hard man like Cullis in tears surely gives the lie to the theory that footballers crying in public is a modern post-Gazza phenomenon. Heartbreak in football is as old as the game itself.

Cullis himself, as we know, rarely spoke of the match again. He had played hard but fair. It may have seemed like a great moral dilemma in the minds of many others who asked him about the incident down the years. There had been no dilemma in his own mind. Two simple sentences sum up Cullis's attitude. He explained: "A lot of people have since asked me why I didn't bring him down or pull Stubbins back by his shirt – and I suppose I could have done. But I didn't want to go down in history as the man who decided the destiny of a championship with a professional foul."

The sportsmanship was applauded in the opposition's paper, the *Liverpool Echo*. Its football writer at the game said in his dispatch: "There was a time when the name of the Wolves at football was linked with a suggestion they could rough it with the best. Liverpool do not subscribe to this: in the latest epoch-making game both sides revelled in sportsmanship and the manner in which Wolves took their severe blow was most praiseworthy."

Winger Johnny Hancocks recalled the day, saying: "That game was one of the saddest I ever played. Everything was set up for Stan Cullis to pick up the League championship trophy in his last game, but it wasn't to be. We had gone to Blackpool to prepare and to escape the supporters, and I remember the great disappointment afterwards. We couldn't get home quickly enough."

Wolves' historian Dr Percy Young was at the game; an incredulous spectator. He wrote: "As I remember it, that match, like others of similar importance, was slightly below standard. That is to say the Wolves players appeared over-anxious and so were not at the peak of their form."

Liverpool themselves had an agonising two-week wait to discover whether their victory at Molineux would deliver the trophy to Anfield. Stoke City's final match away to Sheffield United could not be played until the middle of June because of the fixture backlog and continuing Government restrictions. Stoke had been contenders all season, inspired by the mesmeric skills of Stanley Matthews, even though the great winger was in dispute with the club manager Bob McGrory. A few weeks from the end of the campaign Matthews was controversially sold to Blackpool and Stoke proceeded to lose that final match 2-1 at Bramall Lane to hand the Championship to Liverpool. "Who knows if my presence in the Stoke team might have swung things their way that day," said Matthews modestly. "It is not for me to say."

While this Stanley continued to play for another amazing eighteen years until past the age of fifty, the other great Stanley of English football hung up his boots. It is almost as astonishing to consider that Cullis, captain of England, played only six seasons of League football in his professional career. At the age of thirty he transferred to a tiny office just off the long main corridor in the bowels of the main stand at Molineux.

Joe Baker, the Wolves chairman, kept his promise to make

Cullis the club's assistant manager. Poor Vizard must have known that he was only keeping the seat in the dug-out warm for another man. Even when Vizard had been appointed back in 1944 the rumours had already been gusting around Wolverhampton that Cullis was the man earmarked for the job.

At first Cullis's role was to travel round the country on scouting missions, searching for new talent on small grounds anywhere that a youngster had been recommended. Whether it took him to Ellesmere Port we do not know. Soon his duties were expanded to take charge of the reserve side who were struggling in the Central League. "At last I was able to put into practice some of the lessons I had learned from Major Buckley and during my experiences with England in the war years," said Cullis. "As the reserves began to climb to the top of the Central League table, I felt reasonably confident that I understood some of the basic elements necessary to be a football manager."

The reserves were utterly transformed by the Cullis methods, and finished the season in third place. Any lingering doubts in the Wolves boardroom about whether so young a man could be manager of one of the great clubs of the land had been swept away. There had for a long time been reservations about the way Vizard handled the strong characters of the dressing-room, and even though his team finished fifth in the First Division table in the 1947-48 season and were the top scorers in the Championship for the second successive season, it was the end for the kindly Welshman, who later managed a pub in Wolverhampton, not far from Molineux.

Vizard took the team on a tour of Holland and France in the summer of 1948, but on their return he quit as manager. The reported version was a disagreement with the Board "over policy", but more likely is that it was a move engineered by the directors who had already shown a capacity for manipulation. Just eleven days later Stan Cullis was announced as the new manager of Wolves. It was a surprise to no-one in a town celebrating 100 years since its incorporation as a borough.

A new era had dawned for the town and club. The two became almost synonymous for the next decade as the Iron Manager forged one of the greatest sides in the history of the English game.

Chapter Six

Obsession

"...we took his verbal lashings knowing that they were an outlet for the torture he suffered..." Dennis Wilshaw

ANYONE unfortunate enough to sit next to Stan Cullis the manager at a football match remembered the experience forever. He kicked every ball, crashed into every tackle, headed every cross away from danger – and even sitting in the directors' box or the dug-out his arms and elbows would be working overtime just as they had when he was out on the pitch playing for Wolves and England.

So many people have tales to tell about the most uncomfortable seat in the ground. Bobby Mason, a fine inside-forward at Molineux in the late 1950s, vividly recalled the night he was accidentally parked on the bench next to Cullis in a European Cup away leg against the East German club Vorwaerts. "He kicked me and elbowed me throughout the game," said Mason. "The German crowd found this funny, but not Stan. He turned round angrily and said to them, 'I flopping fought you in the war and I'll flopping fight you now!'. I am sure he meant it too."

Even his young son Andrew didn't escape the Cullis treatment. "I watched many matches with him and sitting next to my father was a complete nightmare," he said. "He was living the game in his seat and if you were next to him you would be kicked to bits. It was his instinctive reaction. There were times in the directors box when suddenly there would be a great yell from someone. Invariably it was because they were sitting next to Stan. As time went by, the seats beside him were often left empty. He was very intense during matches. I was even kicked by him watching schoolboy football."

Cullis was often told about the problem, but he couldn't help himself. In *All For The Wolves*, he wrote: "George Noakes, our chief scout, said he had to go to the treatment room for attention after he had been watching a game next to me. Joe Gardiner, the trainer, told me I pushed him off the bench completely on three occasions when we played Leicester in the 1949 FA Cup Final. No manager worth his salt can escape from the mental tension of a Saturday afternoon, but I envy those like Matt Busby who must feel all the emotions and strains which I feel in a match and show no signs of stress. I am not built like that. You can change your shirt every day but you can't change your nature."

Football, whether as a player or manager, was all or nothing for Stan Cullis. That passion, many would call it an obsession, was at the heart of his character and the heart of his success.

Billy Walker, a famous rival manager with Nottingham Forest in the 1950s, and a man who had played many times against Cullis, summed up this formidable character, saying: "Stan was a young man with every confidence in himself, a natural technical and strategic ability. He was never one to hang back when there was an opinion to be expressed. He had a command of his colleagues that would have sat more easily on an older man. He was a relentless driver of players and he was as determined to have the players conform to his concept of the way Wolves should play, as Major Buckley before him. Stan Cullis learned in a tough hard school, and he was as tough and hard as any of his contemporaries."

His mentor, Major Frank Buckley, the manager who signed him for Wolves, knew very quickly he had a leader of men. Buckley made Cullis captain of a leading First Division team at the age of nineteen, and only a couple of years later was already offering advice to the youngster about the tricks of the management trade, including a lecture on never attempting to reward players with illegal under-the-counter payments. Throughout his young football career, as we have seen, responsibility was thrust at Cullis. England made him their youngest skipper at the age of 22, while the army promoted him quickly in the war and utilised the leadership potential too.

When did Cullis decide he would become a manager? It was probably some time during the war; when he suffered further head injuries, when he discussed the arts and crafts of football for long hours with Matt Busby out in Italy, when he received letters from Wolverhampton cajoling him in that direction. He must certainly have discussed the idea with Buckley, who acted as the middle-man for the approach by Hull City in the summer of 1946. By then there was no doubt where his future lay, with the Wolves board of directors surreptitiously beginning the process of moving Cullis into the role at Molineux.

With the benefit of hindsight it appears inevitable that Cullis would thrive in management. But it cannot have seemed so to him at the time. Cullis became one of the great managers not simply due to a natural suitability for the role as one of life's sergeant-majors, but thanks to the intense effort, thought and dedication he put into the job, much of it even before there was an actual job to do.

Cullis watched everything in the game with acute interest from the moment he walked into Molineux as a novice teenager. He noted how players reacted to commands, how directors had to be confronted when they tried to interfere, how rotten apples in the dressing-room could quickly spread raging discontent, how weak management led to a sense of drift at a club. He learned much in the army days, too; how to organise and pick teams, how to get the best out of men in difficult circumstances, when to shout in anger and when to leave people in peace, how vital the simple fact of mental and physical fitness was to any activity.

"My wartime experiences taught me that proper training can cause the abnormal achievement to become a normal one," remembered Cullis. "Thus, the man who could not walk a mile with a shopping basket in 1939 was often marching ten miles at a smart pace with a hefty load on his back by 1943."

The quest to learn began, as with so much in life, in childhood. Cullis attended many evening classes in various subjects in an effort to better himself and to improve his lot. The same was true in his approach to the game, both purely as a player, and in the years prior to fulfilling his destiny as a manager. Stan Cullis was only 31 years old when Wolves put him in charge of a side in which many of the players had until recently been team-mates. In his mind and outlook, though, Cullis was already a far more experienced man, and he came to the job with many definite principles and ideas already formed.

Cullis once said of his first manager at Wolves: "Buckley was a one-man band, a man who knew exactly what he wanted and where he was going." He might just as well have been talking about himself.

The moment Cullis took control he insisted all the first-team squad gather together for a meeting. This was just thirteen months after Wolves' hopes of winning the 1946-47 Championship had been fatally affected by problems in the dressing-room, problems that Cullis as captain had been unable to influence. Billy Wright later remembered word for word a stirring passage from the kind of speech Cullis naturally knew just when and how to deliver. The new manager said:

> "I want us to see eye to eye right from the start. I want, and I am going to get, one hundred per cent effort from you all, both on and off the field. If I get this support you can take it from me I will be one hundred per cent behind you. Nothing else is going to be enough."

The Cullis creed was set in stone, and he never wavered from it during the next sixteen years at Molineux. Total commitment to the cause brought total loyalty to a player from the Iron Manager. Lack of effort brought a swift and often miserable exit from the Wolves. The words which ring out from the speech are: *"And I am going to get."* There was no question to be asked, no opposition to be brooked. One man was in charge, a man who knew how he would run his club, and knew absolutely the targets he wanted to reach. Those targets were the League Championship title and the FA Cup; both denied to him as a player when glory had looked certain in a number of seasons.

To achieve the success he craved, Cullis was convinced three separate elements essential to a winning football team had to be put in place, a kind of holy trinity of soccer management. He put it like this: "No club can hope to succeed in the tough competition of football unless the players combine in their personality three principal factors. They must have tremendous team spirit, they must be superbly fit, and they must use the correct tactics on the field."

Spirit and fitness and tactics. It is important, I believe, to deal with each element in depth to make a proper assessment of the management philosophy of Stan Cullis, a philosophy that simplistic histories of the game glibly label as "long-ball football".

Yes, it was football which thrived on long passes from defence to attack, football unashamedly based on percentage play. But it was much more than that too; it had to be for a club to achieve so much consistent success through the 1950s.

The season which Cullis enjoyed most was in 1957-58. Wolves won the League Championship, the Central League, the FA Youth Cup, the Birmingham League title, the Worcestershire Combination and the Worcestershire Combination Cup. Only the FA Cup was missing from a complete set of titles from top to bottom of all the sides representing the Wolves. That, for Cullis, was vindication of the 'club spirit' which he tried to instil at Molineux from the lowliest young apprentice to captain Billy Wright heading for a record 100 England caps.

There were many factors which helped create and maintain this 'spirit'. One vital aspect was the benefit payment system of the time, which rewarded players for long service with a club. After five years with a team a player was allowed to receive up to a maximum of £750. Cullis ensured that every footballer who had served the five years and given his all was given the full £750, even if he was a reserve who hardly ever made the first team. At many other clubs that kind of player would receive a much reduced benefit, causing antagonism in the ranks. A classic example at Molineux was a winger called Malcolm Clews who played just one match in the first team but nevertheless was handed his £750 because he had fulfilled his side of the bargain set by the manager.

Cullis ensured that all his players were treated with care, and another example of this came when Eddie Stuart, who had only just joined the club from South Africa, fell ill during the 1952-53 season. He had developed a mysterious infection that a number of doctors could not diagnose, and at one stage his life was thought to be at risk. The club spent a huge amount of money sending Stuart to specialists who eventually diagnosed the problem, and they also flew Stuart's mother over from South Africa.

Attention to small details was vital, thought Cullis. He ensured the players had clean and well-kept dressing-rooms; he demanded they always had new kit. He had a new training ground and pitch built at Castlecrofts. When the club bought houses for players, the manager insisted they were all of similar size so that discontent did not spread. He wanted equality of treatment and justice for all his men, not just extra perks for the stars of the moment. It was a streak of his puritanism and a streak of dazzling common sense.

Cullis may have been a manager with a rasping tongue and a fierce intensity that spilled over into obsession. But he was always fair with the players – and they appreciated it.

Consider the verdict of England midfielder Eddie Clamp, given in 1965 to the *People* newspaper. Clamp said: "Stan Cullis was the hardest character I came across in soccer. And believe me, I saw some tough nuts. With Cullis grown men shivered at the sound of his feet. I suppose you might say my ten-year partnership with the Iron Man was successful. I won international caps, three Championships and a Cup winners' medal. But I'm sure he didn't like me – and I certainly didn't like him. I'll tell you one thing, though. I respected him. I sat scores of times in the dressing-rooms while tough, fit professional players waited nervously. And above the tramp, tramp of his steps in the stone corridor outside I could hear the flat Cullis voice chanting: 'I... will... not... have... a... coward... in... my... team.' One day we beat Newcastle reserves 5-0 in a nothing match and for some strange reason it was a result that delighted Cullis. When we reached Newcastle station he hurried to the sweet stall and bought every player a box of Black Magic. In ten years it was the only present he ever gave me."

Respect and fear and awe and a little uncertainty mingled in the players' minds as they worked for Cullis. That was how he wanted it – and why, no doubt, he kept a cutting of Clamp's summary of life at Molineux in his collection. Other managers would have been outraged by such an article. Cullis saw it as a terrific compliment.

Another player who testified to the never-ending emphasis on club spirit was centre-forward Dennis Wilshaw, a player who also won England caps as well as trophies galore at Molineux. He said: "Never did I know him verbally lash a player whose skill had broken down in a game – but I did hear him give some tremendous lashings to players who did not give everything they had when it came to effort.

"He did not swear at any of the staff. He was a non-smoker for a long while. One day I popped in to see him and was amazed he was smoking. I wondered then if the pressure was beginning to catch up with him. During each game he burned up a fantastic amount of nervous energy, for he associated himself with every kick and every movement. His facial expression was always one of anguish as he mentally willed his players to greater effort. He could not relax for hours after a game and his shirts were soaked with sweat. How he has survived the physical and mental strain for so long surprises me, for he never spared himself. He has been described as a tyrant and a bully, but Stan Cullis was a courageous, straightforward, hard-working man. He ran his club with an honesty which does him more credit than his many achievements, for he had to compete with people who would break all the rules in an attempt to succeed. We accepted that he was usually right and we took his verbal lashings knowing that they were an outlet for the torture he suffered. We grew up with him and understood him, as he did us."

Another Wolves stalwart, Bill Slater, is equally adamant that the popular perception of Cullis was very different from his real character, saying: "He had a great sympathy with the players, even if the public image was of this fierce manager. Anyone could go to him with their problems, and he would do his best to help you. I had a job as a lecturer at Birmingham University, which meant I wasn't allowed time off to travel to away matches in Europe. Stan understood that situation, even though it wasn't ideal from his point of view."

Many of the surviving players of the 1950s like Wilshaw and Slater still meet regularly today under the auspices of the Wolverhampton Former Players' Association. They look back on the Cullis era with rare pride and remember how the youthful team would go into the Lyons Corner House after training to share a coffee and to talk incessantly about football. The club spirit was evident on and off the field, and other great sides have similar experiences. Players from the famous Leeds United team of the 1960s and 1970s managed by Don Revie tell the same tales of meeting up after training to talk about the game.

Cullis fostered the spirit in every way he could, taking particular emphasis in telling the players how important they were to the life of the town. Years later he recalled the attitude of winger Jimmy Mullen, saying: "He gave everything for the club and was always willing to sacrifice his private time for charity work. If I was asked to provide a player for a hospital visit or to open a garden fête, Jimmy was always among the first to volunteer. I needed the players to be good at things other than football, like acting as ambassadors for the town and being part of the community."

One of the hardest moments of Cullis's managerial life was to tell the great Billy Wright that his playing days might be up. He felt it was made a little easier because of the spirit at Molineux, what he called "the atmosphere of mutual trust between club and player." Wright, then 35-years-old, had returned from an England tour of South America in the summer of 1959, having just won his

105th international cap, at the time regarded as a phenomenal world record. Cullis felt Wright might not last the full season ahead, and gently told the England skipper so, while also saying that he would never impose the indignity of demoting Wright to the reserves. Three days later Wright came back to announce that he would retire from football.

"The task of telling Bill I could no longer guarantee him a first-team place was most painful," said Cullis. "Yet I should have been failing in my duty to Wolves if I had failed to do that. I have always told my players that the better man always goes into the senior team. If I had made an exception, even for Wright, the effect would not have been good on morale and spirit at the club. And in the end it is the feeling of the players, the heart they put into the game, and the pride they feel in themselves and their club, which counts."

If spirit was one of three cornerstones of success, equally important was the outstanding fitness and stamina of the players. Buckley had made that a huge virtue of the pre-war Wolves with his weirdly named new gadgets and the monkey gland injections. Cullis also saw vividly at first hand during the war how fitness could improve a man's capacity for achievement. He made the issue another never-ending obsession at Molineux, beginning in pre-season with nightmare military-style runs at full pelt up the steep hills on the heathland of nearby Cannock Chase. It was a torture for the players on a circuit of three hills, each of which had to be climbed three times at speed.

The result was that Wolves were never out-run during a football match, and, as half-back Bill Shorthouse recalled: "We often hit winners in the last minute of games." In the famous Honved match Wolves came from 2-0 down at half-time on a muddy morass of a pitch to win 3-2. Supreme fitness was perhaps even more essential that evocative night than either the spirit in the side or the long-ball strategy.

Cullis employed Frank Morris, a former AAA champion and an international runner, to supervise the fitness training schedule. Each of the players was given imposing personal athletic targets to achieve:

100 yards in 10.5 secs.
220 yards in 24.0 secs.
440 yards in 55.0 secs.
880 yards in 2 mins 5 secs.
1 mile in 4 mins 50 secs.
3 miles in 15 mins 45 secs.
6 miles in 34 mins.
High jump – 4ft 9ins.

The manager reckoned that most players who came to the club could reach those times within eighteen months of arriving at Molineux. The object was to ensure his team could always play at a higher tempo than the opposition side and force them into mistakes. He was also convinced that supreme physical fitness increased the mental agility and awareness of footballers too, enabling them to make better decisions at moments of extreme stress during matches. Wolves players had to "move quickly and think quickly" said Cullis.

Weight-training was introduced at Molineux when it was a novelty rather than the norm. Cullis was always an innovator, whether you agreed with his ideas or not, and he always wanted a scientific approach to the business of football. So, too, did the team widely regarded as the greatest soccer side in history, the Brazilians of Pelé and Gerson and Jairzinho in 1970. Their incomparable talent was underpinned by the most rigorous fitness programme football has ever seen.

"I cannot stress too often that the three great virtues of soccer are spirit, tactics and fitness," said Cullis. "And the greatest of these three might easily be fitness. People used to say that I was an iron-man as a manager. But I had a principle that the players were representing the town of Wolverhampton as well as just Wolverhampton Wanderers. It was their duty to acknowledge that and, for that reason, they had to work hard. I'm sure our training schedule was as hard as anyone's in the country – and it paid off."

The scientific outlook of Cullis was not just concerned with raw fitness. He also wanted specific treatment to eradicate faults he perceived in players. Eddie Clamp was considered to play in a "stiff and unrelaxed" manner when he broke into the first team. He was given a course of exercises to improve his running posture. Cullis noticed that striker Jimmy Murray always landed on one foot after heading the ball and was consequently off-balance and slow to recover his position. Murray went through intensive sessions of pole-vaulting and high-jumping that taught him to land on two feet.

Players who rebelled against the punishing regime at Molineux did not last long at the club. Many like Clamp may have cursed privately at the severity of the discipline and training, but they also understood and reaped the benefits of it.

Cullis never let up on his players. His mantra was, 'There is no substitute for hard work' and he believed it absolutely. Perhaps the most vital part of his role as manager was to make the players believe too. If the players were unwilling to work for the common cause a manager would soon lose his job.

A newspaper article Cullis wrote in the mid-1950s at the height of the worries about English football after the two heavy international defeats to Hungary, illustrates his views perfectly. He said: "I blame the players of today for the decline in our international football prestige. The rot set in at club level. We must correct it at club level. I know what my critics will say when I talk of my playing days. I suppose every old player believes the football was better in his time. But the results prove my point.

"This is why. The players of yesteryear came from the "put-the-coats-down-and-play-anywhere" type of schoolboy. They went on to dedicate themselves to the mastery of ball control. They raced from the pits and the factories mad keen to make the grade as professional footballers. Today your club-man is often indifferent whether or not he plays football.

"THERE IS NO SUBSTITUTE FOR HARD WORK. Put that sign above the dressing-room of every club in the land and we will get soccer back on the road to recovery. I remember the astounded look on the face of one League manager when I told him my boys came back in the afternoon for more training. I might as well have told him I was about to set the boardroom on fire.

"THERE IS NO SUBSTITUTE FOR HARD WORK. Look at

Hungary. I believe their experts have studied tactics all over the world. Above all, they have backed this by a supreme will to make a team of eleven masterly ball players, trained to a peak of physical fitness. Let England take a lesson. Let us work out new tactics with the analytical skill of a science laboratory. Let us evolve a research system in every club that puts every mistake on the field under a microscope. THERE IS NO SUBSTITUTE FOR HARD WORK."

The gospel-like evangelism became even more pronounced when Cullis talked about the final element of his footballing trinity – tactics. While a passionate belief in 'spirit' and 'fitness' could be widely understood and shared, his undying devotion to the long-ball strategy provoked endless controversy. It has never stopped, right through to modern disciples at international level like Graham Taylor with England, Jack Charlton with the Republic of Ireland, and Egil Olsen with Norway.

Football purists almost spit in derision at mention of the long-ball game today – and the hostility to his methods back in the 1950s could be just as fierce. The debate raged across Britain and Europe as Cullis's Wolves won numerous trophies and prestige victories against continental visitors like Honved and Real Madrid.

Cullis as a player could be a daredevil artist. He would perform tricks and dangerous manoeuvres inside his own penalty area that alarmed team-mates. He was an attacking centre-half with an accurate pass, short or long. Although the 1930's manager Major Buckley was a strong critic of 'no conclusion' skills and tricks on the ball, his team did not play what would be generally considered long-ball style. Certainly, it was not the case that Stan Cullis inherited the tactics with which he became so closely associated, and nor were they a natural extension of the way he played the game himself.

So how and when did his reliance on 'long-ball' football come about? In his book *All For The Wolves*, which for the most part is a passionate defence of his football ideas, Cullis set out the reasons why he adopted those tactics for his team. A variety of factors played on his mind – the lack of quality footballers in the immediate post-war years, the problems of playing in the harsh

English winter climate, and the simple desire to score as many goals as possible in every game. Cullis tells how in the four years between the end of the war and 1950 he made an intensive personal study of all the tactics used by Division One clubs. He was a man thirsty for knowledge and information, and the conclusion Cullis drew was the basis of his 'long-ball' soccer.

"Basically," wrote Cullis, "we rely on a framework of tactics which gives ample scope to the operation of the law of averages in football. The number of scoring chances which will arrive during the course of a match is in direct proportion to the amount of time the ball spends in front of goal. If the defenders in the Wolves' team delay their clearances, the ball will be in front of our goal for too long a period and the scoring chances will go to the other side. If too much time is spent in building up our own attacks the ball will spend less of the game in the other team's penalty area and, of course, we shall score fewer goals. Logically, this premise could not be more simple, and it provides the foundations of every good side, English, Hungarian, Brazilian, Russian or Swedish."

Pure, ice-cold logic led Cullis to the conclusion that moving the ball swiftly upfield with long passes would bring Wolves more goals and more victories. Short crossfield passes were a waste of time, and, moreover, dangerous for the team. His view that this was the most sensible tactic for his side was reinforced by the signal lack of skilful talent, as he saw it, in immediate post-war football, a few examples like Stanley Matthews and Tom Finney apart. That meant playing a speedy, direct style of soccer in which "frills were reduced to a minimum in the search for a maximum amount of efficiency." He added: "If people want to label it 'scientific kick and rush' so be it."

It is similar to the way a ruthless businessman will cut costs to make his firm more profitable and successful by cutting out unnecessary expenses and luxuries. The type of words used by Cullis are instructive: efficiency, logic, science. His approach was clinical; he was a professor of football scientifically investigating the game. If people didn't like his theories that was their business.

Pure, ice-cold Saturday afternoons only strengthened his

opinions. Cullis argued that the treacherous mid-winter pitches of England, muddy or frozen, were inimical to the more artistic football of the Latins. That kind of play became bogged down, he thought. So, on a wholly practical basis again, the long-passing strategy he adopted was the most sensible and the most efficient.

It is useful to note here that Cullis campaigned passionately for many years for a midwinter break from football in January and February, suggesting that English League soccer should be played in the more weather-friendly months of summer. That would mean more skilful English footballers and a general improvement in the quality of play, he said – and his forceful support of this idea helps give the lie to critics who believed he was a one-eyed advocate of kick-and-rush tactics.

Cullis was not. But he was a realist, and he felt that, given all the conditions which prevailed, his ideas and principles were correct. It helped, too, that when he began to use them with Wolves there was immediate reward with a victory in the 1949 FA Cup Final. Managers never like to tinker too much with a winning formula.

His strategy was not long-ball soccer in the modern sense of the term which has come to mean long hoofs upfield and a fight for the second ball. Cullis's theory was accurate long-passing soccer – and there is a profound difference. Modern fans drool over the sublime fifty-yard drilled passes of David Beckham, as they did over Glenn Hoddle in the 1980s.

A tactic which became central to the Wolves team was finding wingers Jimmy Mullen and Johnny Hancocks with long passes from defence. The pair would often sweep majestic diagonal crossfield passes from one to the other. If that pass put the other winger clear of his full-back he would race on goal to shoot. If the full-back was still covering, the second winger would either cross to a forward like Roy Swinbourne or even send a return pass back to the other winger. The ball was always moving forward at high speed, and mostly with the precision which created genuine scoring chances.

Hancocks' passing was incredibly accurate. He once stood on the halfway line during training at Molineux and bet Stan Cullis he could hit the crossbar at least once in six attempts from the halfway line. Cullis, not a gambling man at all, wagered a sixpence and was happy to pay up as Hancocks performed the trick, hitting the bar twice.

Cullis recalled another bet with the winger, saying: "I told him he couldn't beat me with six penalties out of six in training. He took the first two or three and I don't think I even saw them as they screamed into the net. Then, for the fourth, I moved early and had the misfortune to get my hand to it. The ball still went in and I was having treatment off the physio, George Palmer, for a fortnight."

There is, essentially, little difference between Wolves' long-passing game, at its best, and the swift counter-attacking movements of modern teams like Manchester United. But a huge mythology grew up around the Cullis methods, and it was fertile ground for newspapers eager to generate controversy as they sold millions of copies to football fans.

The match which inspired more talk about football tactics than any other in the history of the English game was Hungary's 6-3 defeat of England at Wembley in 1953. The defeat stunned soccer lovers, the way Hungary played shocked them even more. It was as if Ferenc Puskas, Nandor Hidegkuti and the rest of the Magyars were footballers from another planet with their speed and skill and sorcery on the ball.

Most critics were entranced by the swift, short-passing move-ments in midfield that left England's players chasing shadows. Billy Wright was memorably described as being like "a fire engine turning up for the wrong fire" when left mesmerised by Puskas. Cullis saw an entirely different match, and so, totally unknown to him that day, did an anonymous RAF Wing Commander, Charles Reep, sitting elsewhere in the crowd at Wembley.

Cullis watched the Hungarians and marvelled at the wonderfully accurate long passes which also littered their play. That was what he 'wanted' to see, just as the newspaper critics 'wanted' to see the short-passes which they had informed their readers about in the build-up to the match. Cullis noted mentally that only one of the Hungarians' six goals came from a move that started in their own half of the field. Three of the goals came after a movement of only one pass, one came from a movement of two passes, and one direct from a free-kick. One goal out of the six followed a passage of play of seven passes. Cullis also noted how goalkeeper Gyula Grosics kicked the ball long upfield more often than not.

When the Hungarians had the match comfortably won in the second half he observed how they then sat back and played a 'free-wheeling' style of keep-ball in midfield. It looked dazzling, but in fact was merely designed to keep possession away from the England players rather than build Magyar attacks.

Puskas gave his own version on the tactics debate, saying: "In some measure we improved the England saying 'kick and run'. We made it 'pass accurately and run into a good position'. We didn't nurse the ball but kept passing it so quickly that an onlooker might have thought the ball was burning our feet."

Cullis had sat with his Wolves trainer and former 1930s team-mate Joe Gardiner watching the high-tempo brilliance of Puskas and his pals. He said: "We both thought that the play of the Hungarians confirmed most of the ideas we were trying to use at Molineux."

No-one else did, no-one except Wing Commander Reep, who turned up at Molineux to see Cullis shortly after the Wembley game. He was an accountant officer in the RAF, based at nearby Bridgnorth. Reep had devised a statistical method of recording every move in a football match in complete detail, and his analysis of the 6-3 Hungarian victory was similar to that of the Wolves manager. His mathematics backed up the intuition of Cullis, who said: "Reep's recordings of the Hungary match showed in exact detail the principles which I believed to be true. He was able to establish in black and white the facts for which I was forced to trust my memory where, inevitably, some would become lost or confused."

How much Cullis latched on to Reep's work because it was a 'scientific' vindication of his own ideas, and how much because it was of practical use to him is now impossible to say nearly half a century later. But there is no doubt that a bond was quickly formed and the Wolves manager pored over the mountain of statistics that came his way, saying: "It helped me modify and improve points of tactics which were either costing us goals or reducing our own scoring potential." Cullis certainly enjoyed talking up benefits of Reep's theory of POMO – the so-called Position of Maximum Opportunity.

Mathematics and logic are intimately related disciplines, and the statistic which mattered most to Cullis, of course, was the goals scored column in the First Division table. If that was high his team would be challenging for honours, and in Cullis's eyes the more times his team hit the back of the net, the more the fans of Wolverhampton were entertained. He was particularly proud of the fact that they scored more than 100 goals for four seasons in succession.

Of course, every football fan finds entertainment in a game in his own way. Supporters and spectators are thrilled by players dribbling past defenders, they appreciate the skill involved in intricate passing movements, they marvel at moments of magical trickery on the ball. Pele called football 'The Beautiful Game' – with good reason.

Cullis had a deep love of the game, and he admired high skill in football players. But he was insistent that individual talent had to be harnessed for the common good of the team and had to serve an efficient function. There was no value to him in art for art's sake, yet his Wolves' teams possessed a number of skilful ballplayers and natural crowd entertainers like Peter Broadbent, Jimmy Murray and Bobby Mason.

The published views of the Iron Manager on this issue can be contradictory. A famous line often quoted against him was: "Because we insist that every player in possession of the ball makes rapid progress towards the business of launching an attack, our forwards are not encouraged to parade their abilities in ostentatious fashion which might please a small section of the crowd at a cost of reducing the efficiency of movement."

Compare that to this Cullis homily: "Peter Broadbent was a classic, the kind of player you allowed to express himself and entertain the public. After all, he had balance, and you cannot be a very good player without that. Perhaps he lacked a little determination, I don't know. I do know the £7,500 I paid for him was one of the best things I ever did."

The truth perhaps lies somewhere in between these two contrasting statements. Billy Wright was the captain of Wolves throughout the golden decade and this was his view: "Some ill-advised critics called it kick and rush. Nothing could be further from the truth. Every phase is strictly logical and, although placing unselfish co-ordination before individualism, Cullis has never scorned ball players. Forwards like Broadbent and Murray are essentially craftsmen in possession of the ball, and all found tremendous scope for their talents within the broad framework of Wolves long-ball game."

Modern commentators on the game with an intimate knowledge of the time agree that the long-ball tag is a myth.

Ron Atkinson, a groundstaff boy at Molineux in the mid-1950s had this view: "The tactics weren't long ball, but long passing. There were extremely talented players, but the wing-half knew he was not allowed to pass the ball square. That would bring down Stan's wrath in a big way. He thought that was a very negative way of playing. Cullis was a great thinker about the game. He was one of the first to have fitness and sprint trainers. They had this ability to wear teams down with their physical presence."

One of the great midfielders, Johnny Giles, played against Wolves at youth and first-team level. He is known for his purist views on how football should be played, and said: "The Wolves style was not long-ball in the way that we think of it now. Yes, it was direct, but the passes were played with a purpose to reach the wingers Hancocks and Mullen. The passes were played to feet, not into space. That would have been no good for the wingers. And it is also the case that they had very skilful players like Broadbent. That is my lasting memory of playing against them."

If Wolves did not quite match other teams like Manchester United's Busby Babes or Arthur Rowe's 'push-and-run' Spurs title-winning team of 1950 for pure skill, they compensated with spirit and fitness and a tactical plan that worked for them.

They also had a manager who worked ceaselessly to improve

performance. There were team-talks that could last anything from twenty minutes to an hour and a half in which Cullis would use a large blackboard with magnetic figures to explain what he wanted, Every player would come under Professor Cullis's microscope as he talked in simple, clear language about the next game. Criticisms could he harsh, but there was always a constructive point to what was said.

For all the success that long-ball tactics brought to his Wolves team, Cullis never ceased in his desire to learn about the game. He made various trips to the other side of the Iron Curtain to study the methods of the Russians and Hungarians. He marvelled at the palatial facilities built for the players of Moscow Dynamo.

When the 1958 World Cup was staged in Sweden, a tournament which saw seventeen-year-old Pele explode on to the scene as Brazil won the Final 5-2, Cullis travelled round assessing the revolutionary new 4-2-4 tactics beginning to be employed. While Cullis stayed in smart hotels, another intelligent soccer man, Dave Sexton, spent the tournament sleeping on campsites as he continued the soccer education which would make him a fine manager years later.

Cullis had a few managerial tricks up his sleeve too. In games at Molineux he would always ensure that the opposing team went out on to the field first, to leave the 55,000 crowd waiting in anticipation to unleash a huge roar for their team and hopefully intimidate their rivals. When Joe Mercer became a manager and brought his various teams to the Wolves' ground, he knew all about this and tried a game of bluff. The two schoolboy pals from Ellesmere Port would be like little kids keeping look-out through a crack in their dressing-room doors waiting for the other team to walk up the corridor on to the pitch first.

An understanding of player psychology was a vital part of Cullis's management. The famous bone-trembling tirades against a slacking player at half-time in a match should be set against occasions when he knew sympathy or silence was required. Billy Wright recalled how Cullis reacted during the 1949 FA Cup semi-final against Manchester United, when both Wolves full-backs were injured in the first half. He said: "The tension was unworldly, and at half-time a wrong word or action would have sent us to pieces. Stan sensed that nothing but encouragement was needed and said exactly the right things. He showed us that day what a great manager he was." There were no substitutes in those days, but Wolves gallantly survived and won the replay to reach Wembley, where they lifted the Cup in Cullis's first season as a manager.

How vital were those few half-time minutes in establishing the legend of Stan Cullis the manager? And how different was his attitude that day to the image and the myths that surround him?

Wright said: "Stan was a forceful character and possessed tremendous personality and punch. He had that priceless ability to make those surrounding him produce their best form. He was a hard man to please, never completely satisfied with himself. I would not be telling the truth if I said Stan Cullis and I always agreed. There were times when I thought, and told him, that I considered he was wrong. But we had a warm regard for the integrity of each other. Cullis was a football thinker, and he also encouraged others to think hard about the game. This outstanding trait plus his tremendous drive puts him among the great leaders. Managers should be a leader of men – and I feel I became a better man than I would have been for working with Cullis."

Cullis had a Jekyll and Hyde character, according to Wright. During the week his managerial door was always open to anyone from a first-team regular to the youngest apprentice who wanted to talk football. On Saturdays the obsession took hold of him. "Stan was a man possessed in a game," recalled Wright, "and it was at half-time that his passions seemed to reach a climax. Winning was so important to him that in the drama of the moment he was liable to say or do anything."

After a game there were three different reactions Cullis might adopt. If he said 'well done' the players knew he was very pleased. Alternatively he might burst into the dressing-room, win lose or draw, and in a raging temper begin to tear the team's performance apart with ruthless criticism. Worst of all, though, was a heavy defeat. Then Cullis was so angry that he would stomp past the players into the physio's room, almost unable to speak. That left the team trembling. "We knew he would find the appropriate words before very long," said Wright.

Sometimes that might be on the coach or train home from a match, a journey which could feature hours of discussions and analysis of that afternoon's game. It could be a tougher fixture than the football itself for some players.

Sportswriter David Miller, who played for the famous amateur side Pegasus in the 1950s, also noted that Cullis could be hard with young footballers. He said: "Stan could be a bully at times. It was a tactic that didn't always work, with Alan Hinton, for example, a winger who would later enjoy much success under Brian Clough at Derby County."

The intensity of Cullis's management did put strains on his health. He had to take a month's rest after the 1956 season on medical advice, and had been away recuperating for three weeks before being sacked by Wolves in 1964. When Billy Wright gave his insightful assessment of the character of Cullis in 1961, shortly after leaving the club, he said: "There were times when I became really worried about Stan's health, that if he continued to be carried away so completely by the game he would eventually have a breakdown. Thankfully, his health has been robust, but even now he finds it hard to relax completely and it must be very difficult for his wife Winifred to find ways of making him forget all about football."

It was impossible to do that. The game consumed Stan Cullis. His daughter Susan has a telling memory from his childhood that illustrates the point, saying: "He was very single-minded about his football and was rarely at home. There was one occasion when we sat down for tea and my mother said she didn't know where my father was, she did not have a clue. We switched on the TV news and there was a clip showing him and the Wolves team getting on a plane that afternoon to fly out to Europe somewhere. My mother knew nothing about it at all. It was an example of the eccentric side of his nature, and of the fact that football took over his life."

Chapter Seven

Flying the Flag

"...Wolves restored my confidence in the British style of play..." Charles Buchan

I N THE parish church closest to Molineux flowers were planted in the grass to spell out 'Champions - Bravo Wolves'. The floral tribute to the football team which restored English football prestige in a series of compelling victories against foreign foe was a display of civic pride by the town. "It told what and where Wolverhampton worships," wrote the famous and perceptive newspaperman J. L. Manning.

Praise showered on Stan Cullis's team for their continental exploits came in may forms; the church flowers, telegrams from the House of Commons, Fleet Street eulogies, and the creation of the European Cup itself. It is little wonder that Cullis considered the victory against Honved, in particular, his finest hour.

Wolves had been playing overseas teams from the early 1930s onwards, just before Cullis joined the club. In 1933 they went on a tour of France to play against Marseilles, Nice, Racing Club de Paris and Nimes. The match in Nice turned into a roughhouse brawl, manager Major Frank Buckley taking his players off the pitch because of the fighting. He refused to continue the match until extra men from the local gendarmerie were called in to assure order."I have brought my team here to play football, not be slaughtered," said Buckley afterwards. Nevertheless, Nice visited Wolverhampton the next season. Buckley knew what would sell tickets.

Cullis first played against foreign opposition when the long-forgotten Pavi Kavatski Gradjanski club from Yugoslavia visited Molineux. Wolves won the match 4-2, but only 646 people watched on a foggy afternoon. It was a far cry from the atmospheric nights of packed crowds watching under floodlights when Honved and Real Madrid visited in the 1950s, or even the 7-2 army triumph against the Yugoslav partizans during the war.

After the war many more of these friendly matches against exotic visitors were staged. One effect of world war had been huge technological advances in all areas. Airline travel became routine with the invention of the jet engine, making lightning trips across Europe to play football matches attractive and feasible. The days of England or club players travelling round the continent on the Orient Express or a steamer down the Danube had gone forever.

In November 1946 Wolves beat the Swedish side Norrkoping. This time there was a crowd of more than 30,000 at the game. Other early post-war opponents at Molineux were the South African national side, who were beaten 3-1, and Maccabi Tel Aviv from Israel, thrashed 10-1. They were, however, merely hors d'oeuvres before a meatier main course as the lights went up at Molineux.

The floodlights arrived at the ground in September 1953, specifically ordered by Cullis, who knew they represented an integral part of the future of football. While his on-field tactics may have been derided for their lack of invention, he revelled in bringing every new innovation to the club. The towering pylons with powerful bulbs to light up dark nights cost £25,000, and Cullis personally supervised their installation. Linesman's flags were equipped with natty little electric lights in their handles so the crowd could more easily spot offsides being called.

The old gold shirts of the Wolves were made in a special new silky, fluorescent material that glowed brightly in the dark and made the players appear like darting fireflies racing around the pitch, well it did at least in the vivid imagination of some of the soccer writers of the day. The players themselves found the shirts a nuisance because they would ride up their backs rather than hang down normally, but it all added to the magic and mystique of these new midweek night matches.

"Those lights were something special," Cullis remembered. "It was as if an electric fuse reached all the way round the ground."

A month after they were installed at Wolverhampton, a dark gloom descended over the nation's football in general when Hungary won 6-3 against England at Wembley. The humiliating defeat was England's first ever at home in an international match and brought an avalanche of recrimination and soul-searching.

Cullis's verdict on that landmark afternoon was very different from most observers. For him it was a vindication of his own principles rather than reason for despondency. His beliefs did not cut too much ice with others, not even when Wolves won the League Championship that season. However, there were one or two influential voices of support, notably that of the famous old England star of the 1920s, Charles Buchan, who had become one of the leading football writers of the day, with a famous soccer magazine named after him.

"Wolves restored my confidence in the British style of play in a victory against Spurs," wrote Buchan in the News Chronicle a few weeks after the 6-3 debacle. "They were fast, direct, and played to a plan every bit as good as that of the Hungarians at Wembley. Wolves matched the continentals in pace and ball control. Their defence particularly impressed me. It was the type England will need in the World Cup. Close marking and quick tackling cut to ribbons the 'push-and-run' methods of the Spurs forwards. I am certain, too, that the direct wing play of Johnny Hancocks and Jimmy Mullen would set a problem to the continental defenders. There is great chance for England in the World Cup if it is carried out on the Wolves pattern."

The England football selectors ignored Buchan's advice. When England made a return visit to Budapest in the spring of 1954 the

The young Stan Cullis in thoughtful pose in a Wolves shirt.

Leading out the Wolves, both knees heavily bandaged.

Cullis shakes hands with Sheffield United skipper Harry Hooper before the FA Cup fourth-round tie at Molineux in January 1937.

Greetings again, this time between Cullis and the Grimsby Town captain before the 1939 FA Cup semi-final at Old Trafford.

Cullis introduces the Wolves team to King George VI before the 1939 FA Cup Final against Portsmouth at Wembley.

Each player on the England summer tour of 1939 was presented with a souvenir itinerary. Among other things it told them that 'shirts, knickers and stockings' would be provided but that 'a supply of toilet soap should be taken'.

England players pictured outside their Milan hotel in May 1939. Cullis sports a checked coat. To the extreme right of the photograph are Tommy Lawton and Frank Broome.

Leading out England for the first time, against Romania in Bucharest in May 1939.

Exchanging floral bouquets with the Romanian skipper. Cullis led his country to a 2-0 victory.

Cullis introduces Sheffield United's Jimmy Hagan to Clement Attlee before a wartime international at Wembley. To Hagan's right is Stoke's Stanley Matthews, then Raich Carter of Sunderland and George Hardwick of Middlesbrough.

International stars pictured before a Scotland-England game at Glasgow in 1944. Cullis takes a sideways glance at Manchester City goalkeeper Frank Swift. Sitting next to Swift is Jimmy Hagan. Joe Mercer has a hand on Cullis's shoulder. Tommy Lawton is standing behind Swift. Raich Carter is the RAF sergeant sitting to the left of the picture.

On manoeuvres? Stan Cullis in full marching kit, rifle and all.

Cullis's first managerial job, in charge of 176 Squadron RAF Rest Camp team against a Yugoslavian XI at Bari in September 1944.

The captain of Wolves and the captain of Everton. Stan Cullis and Joe Mercer shake hands at Goodison Park.

In later years the two good friends, Cullis and Mercer, visiting a sports goods factory.

Training at Molineux. Cullis with Joe Gardiner (left) and Tom Galley (centre).

Cullis bows his head when meeting the Duke of Edinburgh before the 1949 FA Cup Final against Leicester City.

With skipper Billy Wright, admiring the trophy after Leicester were beaten 3-1.

A beautifully-lit tableau in the Wolves dressing-room, photographed for *John Bull* magazine.

Blackboard lesson for Wolves players, again set up especially for the photographer.

A quiet word at half-time with Bill Slater, the last amateur to play in an FA Cup Final, when he was with Blackpool.

A word with Peter Broadbent under a piece of training apparatus at Molineux, designed for practising heading.

The League Championship trophy found its way to Molineux three times in the 1950s.

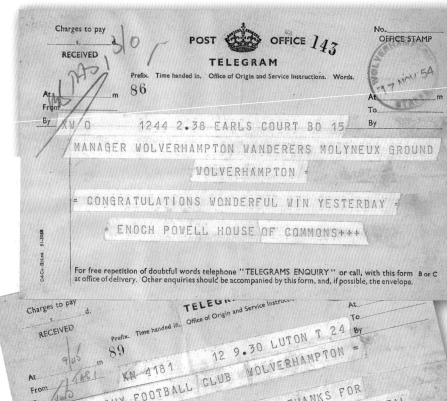

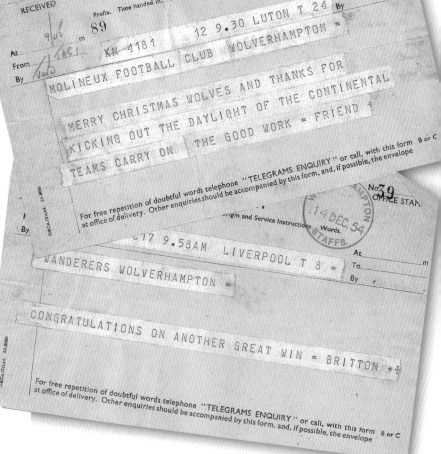

Congratulatory telegrams, including one from local MP Enoch Powell, after another win over European opposition in 1954.

POST OFFICE 143 TELEGRAM

Charges to pay

s. d.

RECEIVED

Prefix. Time handed in. Office of Origin and Service Instructions. Words.

86

At From m

By XW O 1244 2.38 EARLS COURT BO 15

No.

OFFICE STAMP

17 NOV 54

At To m

By

MANAGER WOLVERHAMPTON WANDERERS MOLYNEUX GROUND

WOLVERHAMPTON =

= CONGRATULATIONS WONDERFUL WIN YESTERDAY =

= ENOCH POWELL HOUSE OF COMMONS+++

For free repetition of doubtful words telephone "TELEGRAMS ENQUIRY" or call, with this form B or C at office of delivery. Other enquiries should be accompanied by this form, and, if possible, the envelope.

Charges to pay

s. d.

RECEIVED

TELEGRAM

Prefix. Time handed in. Office of Origin and Service Instructions.

89

At From

By XN 4181 12 9.30 LUTON T 24 =

MOLINEUX FOOTBALL CLUB WOLVERHAMPTON =

MERRY CHRISTMAS WOLVES AND THANKS FOR

KICKING OUT THE DAYLIGHT OF THE CONTINENTAL

TEAMS CARRY ON THE GOOD WORK = FRIEND +

At To By

For free repetition of doubtful words telephone "TELEGRAMS ENQUIRY" or call, with this form B or C at office of delivery. Other enquiries should be accompanied by this form, and, if possible, the envelope.

14 DEC 54

No. 30 OFFICE STAMP

Origin and Service Instructions. Words.

17 9.58AM LIVERPOOL T 8 =

WANDERERS WOLVERHAMPTON =

CONGRATULATIONS ON ANOTHER GREAT WIN = BRITTON ++

At To m By

For free repetition of doubtful words telephone "TELEGRAMS ENQUIRY" or call, with this form B or C at office of delivery. Other enquiries should be accompanied by this form, and, if possible, the envelope

WOLVES CENTRAL LEAGUE SIDE HAVE AN INSPIRING STRING OF SUCCESSES —

7 WINS IN A ROW

10 MATCHES WITHOUT DEFEAT

35 GOALS IN 10 MATCHES

THEY ARE BENEFITING FROM THE EXPERIENCE OF STAN CULLIS.

ARROWSMITH

Local newspaper cartoonist 'Arrowsmith' marked Wolves Reserves' feats with Cullis, inevitably, pulling the strings.

In charge of the Football League team which met the Scottish League at Ibrox in 1961. It was practically a full England side which included Jimmy Greaves, Bobby Charlton and Bobby Robson.

FA Cup winners again, this time after beating a depleted Blackburn side in a moderate Final at Wembley in 1960.

Two successful West Midlands managers. Stan Cullis of Wolves pictured with Jimmy Hill, the former Fulham player and PFA chief who led the 'Sky Blue Revolution' of Coventry City in the early 1960s.

Handwritten letter of sympathy from Matt Busby after Cullis had been dismissed by Wolves.

Manchester United Football Club Ltd.

M. BUSBY, C.B.E., Manager   L. OLIVE, Secretary

TELEGRAPHIC ADDRESS :
STADIUM, MANCHESTER

TELEPHONE TRAFFORD PARK
1661 & 1662

Old Trafford,
Manchester, 16.
16th Sept. 1964

My Dear Stan,
 I am still trying to recover from the shock of yesterday's announcement. It has knocked me sick of humane nature. How people could do such a thing after you giving them your life's blood? What more success can they get than what you've given them! What loyalty have they shown you after the loyalty you given them in every way! Oh, I could go on and on. Anyway, Stan please accept my sincere sympathies and whatever you decide to do in the future may it abound with happiness and success is the wish of
 Your Friend,
 Matt.

In contra
a brief
typewrit
note ask
Cullis to
return h
keys to
Molineu

WOLVERHAMPTON WANDERERS FOOTBALL CLUB (1923) LIMITED

Telegraphic Address "Wanderers Wolverhampton"

Telephone 24053—4

JOHN R. IRELAND
Chairman

~~STANLEY CULLIS~~
~~*Manager*~~

JOHN T. HOWLEY
Secretary

Registered Office:

Molineux Grounds

Wolverhampton

JTH/JC.

WINNERS OF F.A. CUP, 1892-3, 1907-8, 1948-9, 1959-60.
FINALISTS, 1888-9, 1895-6, 1920-1, 1938-9.
WINNERS FOOTBALL LEAGUE (WAR) CUP, 1941-2
CHAMPIONS—DIV. 1, 1953-4, 1957-8-9.
DIV. 2, 1931-2.
DIV. 3, (NORTHERN SECTION) 1923-4.
CENTRAL LEAGUE 1931-2 1950-1-2-3, 1957-8-9.
RUNNERS-UP—DIV. 1, 1937-8-9, 1949-50, 1954-5, 1959-60.

14th October, 1964.

S. Cullis, Esq.,
"Greenlands",
48, Wrottesley Road,
Tettenhall,
Staffs.

Dear Stan,

I have been instructed
by the Chairman to request you to let
me have your keys of the Club.

Yours sincerely,

Jock

humiliation was far greater. Hungary won the match 7-1 against an England team containing only one player from Wolves – skipper Billy Wright. This is not to suggest that Hancocks and Mullen would have altered the result of that match, but their subsequent performances against Honved are entitled to make us wonder whether Buchan had a valid point about a different English pattern of play being more effective.

An alternative view to this was delivered by Desmond Hackett in Beaverbrook's *Daily Express* in April 1954, a month before the Budapest game. Hackett was a celebrity sports journalist, a man who relished stunts like vowing to eat his famous brown bowler hat if his forceful predictions were proved wrong.

"Wolves are top of the First Division, the supremos of English football," wrote Hackett. "It is possible they may win the League. I hope they do not. They may be the most effective side in the country, but in their determined and single-minded chase for points and goals they have tossed overboard the fine arts of soccer. Wolves went thumping for goals against Charlton. They shattered them with unrelenting thumping tackles; they thumped the ball solidly upfield; they thumped in the their centres; and finally thumped the ball at the unfortunate Charlton goalkeeper Sam Bartram as often as they could. If anyone broke off from this thump-thump practice and sought to play studied football the fans would roar: 'Get it into the goal!' Which is the reason why England football is not half what it used to be. We are producing a player nation of point scrapers and goal chasers."

This was classic Hackett, controversial, opinionated journalism written to provoke either applause or indignant anger among readers. His views, however, could be inconsistent. One month earlier Hackett had given a rather different verdict on Cullis's team in the *Daily Express* in his report of the least considered of Wolves' floodlight victories against foreign visitors, a 3-1 triumph against Racing Club of Buenos Aires on 10 March 1954.

"Wolverhampton Wanderers efficiently demonstrated that English soccer played with speed and spirit is still world class when they mastered Racing Club last night," wrote Hackett. "Wolves played with a pace and a plan that was a joy to watch. The system of long accurate passing broke down the Argentinian aces who had been first or second in their league in the past four seasons."

England reached the quarter-finals of the 1954 World Cup, where they played three matches in the tournament. Belgium were beaten after extra-time in the opening pool game, which was followed by a 2-0 victory against host nation Switzerland. The goals were scored by Wolves pair Jimmy Mullen and Dennis Wilshaw, and set up a quarter-final against reigning world champions Uruguay. This time Mullen was left out in favour of Stanley Matthews, who had recovered from injury and gave a majestic personal display. England played with a combination of short and long passes, Wilshaw twice missing the target by inches at critical moments. Uruguay, eventually, won a thrilling encounter 4-2, but the match brought admiration for the England team.

Here was a ray of hope at a time when the credibility of English football around the world was being widely questioned; its prestige shattered by a series of damning defeats that began with the shocking 1-0 defeat to the USA in the 1950 World Cup tournament in Brazil.

It was against this background that Wolves launched themselves into their floodlit showpiece clashes against the best clubs from Europe. Over the next five years many of the most feared sides travelled to Molineux – and none left in triumph. The ray of hope became a blast of sunshine.

First Vienna were beaten with ease, both at home and away, the Austrians' goalkeeper saying after the first game that Wolves were the best side seen in Vienna since the war. San Lorenzo were another Argentinian club invited over, and they were overwhelmed 5-1 at Molineux.

However, the two matches which became legend were those played against Spartak Moscow in November 1954, and against Honved a month later. They captured the imagination of the whole country both for the compelling drama involved and the thrilling fact of victory. Bryon Butler, the long-serving football correspondent of the BBC, saw many of these matches, and he recalled: "There was something special about Molineux on those dark rainy nights. What was extraordinary was the attitude of the fans to foreign sides. There was a tremendous naivete about it all, almost a feeling that these were men from the moon rather than footballers from another neighbouring European country."

The Spartak fixture was scheduled for a Monday night. That meant Wolves trained on a Sunday for the first time, according to club historian Percy Young, for 77 years. Cullis liked to attend church on Sundays, and although he sometimes conducted essential business on the sabbath, he liked to regard it as his day of rest. That Sunday he worked feverishly to prepare his players for the visit of the club regarded as the best Russian team of the time, with a robust, highly organised and efficient defence.

So it proved. The match was high on tension but low on goalmouth drama as both defences looked impregnable. At half-time the score was 0-0. So it remained until the 80th minute. Then the dam burst as the supremely fit Wolves team notched four goals in the final ten minutes to sweep to an ultimately crushing victory. Winger Johnny Hancocks scored the first two goals, and Roy Swinbourne and Dennis Wilshaw added the others to leave Spartak's goalkeeper, Piraev, a tiny figure with a magnificent drooping moustache, looking a picture of misery as he trooped off the pitch.

Hancocks was a quiet man in the dressing-room, but in a silent moment after the match he quipped: "Well I think I know where that goalie's going – the salt mines!" His team-mates exploded into uncontrollable laughter, and by the time Wolves made a return visit to Moscow the next year Piraev had indeed left Spartak, much to the dismay of Hancocks and company. Thankfully, he had been transferred to Dinamo Tbilisi rather than Siberia.

The result was widely hailed as a triumph for English football values; an understandable if over-stated response to one home friendly victory, however dramatic the occasion. What cannot be over-stated is the morale boost it gave to soccer in particular and to the country in general. Telegrams flooded into Cullis's office at Molineux from all over the country. One that typified the mood was sent by the manager of the Dolphin Hotel in Southampton, which read: "Strongly recommend unsatisfactory England team be scratched and glorious, magnificent, ferocious, goal-hungry

Wolves substituted in entirety for important match against Germany." Wolverhampton's famous Member of Parliament, Enoch Powell, milked the occasion like any shrewd politician would, sending a telegram of congratulation as well.

Floodlit games also made for ideal television viewing in the early days of broadcasting, and BBC commentator Ken Wolstenholme remembers covering the game. He said: "It was quite a foggy night at Molineux which only added to the atmosphere and meant that you could hardly see to the other end of the pitch with the naked eye. Our cameras were at one end of the ground, the wrong end when Wolves were attacking the first half. The score was 0-0 at half-time and then they scored four times at the right end of the pitch for us. People kept asking how much we'd paid the players to fix that for us. It was pure luck on our part."

On the same day that the *Daily Mail's* soccer reporters lauded Wolves for a "wonderful victory for English football", their TV columnist Peter Black was among the first to observe a new social phenomenon that was transforming the daily lives of people in Britain.

He wrote: "A surprising factor has emerged from the two-months run of the BBC's programme *Is this Your Problem?* In common with all the critics I had assumed that those willing to air their worries in front of a television audience must necessarily be the cranks, eccentrics and neurotics of our island race. Huw Wheldon, the producer, tells me that almost without exception they have been sane decent ordinary folk, who have taken their worries to television simply because they see this box in the corner as an authoritative counsellor. Why confide to six million people a story kept secret from the doctor and priest? The explanation I suppose is that, simply by existing, television has broken down the active social life that went on when people made their own fun. A family today can live in the same street for ten years without learning the names of more than half a dozen neighbours, and neighbourly friendship has been replaced by tittle-tattle. It is the box in the corner that is the source of entertainment and conversation."

Life in Britain was changing at a startling pace in the 1950s. Old certainties were disappearing, new innovations arriving all the time. Stan Cullis tapped into this mood most obviously with his floodlit football extravaganzas. But it also informed his whole outlook on the game. He was a man in love with the new, who worked hard on plans for a futuristic Molineux stadium, and who supported ideas like a world club championship and reduced English Premier League that would only arrive nearly forty years later. Cullis was also the first manager to understand how vital the television revolution would be to football, arguing passionately that regular 'live' TV matches would enhance the game and give it access to a huge new income from broadcasting companies. He was almost a lone voice advocating that at a time when the football authorities were deeply fearful of the new medium.

Critics may have derided Stan Cullis's long-ball tactics as old-fashioned. Little else in his sporting life was. And when the direct style brought League championships and famous European victories, why should he worry about the slings and arrows of outrageous columnists.

A month after the Spartak Moscow match the visitors to Molineux were Honved, a club side containing six of the great Hungarian national side which had so comprehensively humiliated England, like Ferenc Puskas and Sandor Kocsis. A stormy December night conjured up one of the most evocative and significant matches in the entire history of football.

Cullis approached the fixture in bullish mood following the victory against the Russians. "I had seen these Hungarians play so often that I was confident I knew the answer to their tactics," he said in the immediate aftermath of Wolves' dramatic 3-2 victory in which they recovered from two goals down at half-time. "You see, in my opinion, these Hungarians have analysed every country's style of play. They have taken bits and pieces from each. They play as I've always wanted my lads to play. They can use the long passes as well as the short ones. We have yet to conquer the short-passing tactics. When we do, I don't think there is a team that will beat us."

Striker Roy Swinbourne, who scored two goals, including the winner, recalled the hype that preceded the fixture, saying: "Wolves never played a match in which there was so much pride involved as the Honved game. The Hungarians had given us such a hammering in the internationals that people built up the club match as an opportunity to show we were still as good as the continentals."

Half-back Bill Slater said: "The Honved match was special because there was so much expectation leading up to the game. It was on the television, which was very unusual at the time, and I remember thinking I might even miss the match because the roads were so thick with people going to the game."

Memories of that night are legion. Ron Atkinson, later to become a celebrated manager himself with the tag 'Big Ron' at clubs like Manchester United and Aston Villa, was a sixteen-year-old apprentice at Molineux back then. He recalled a manoeuvre by Cullis that he felt helped to win the game.

"I'll never forget the Honved game," said Atkinson. "On the morning of the match Stan Cullis sent for me and two of the other apprentices, and told us to get out and water the pitch then roll the moisture in. We thought he was out of his mind; it was December, and it had been raining incessantly for four days. But we groundstaff boys kept pounding the pitch with these big heavy rollers and it was only when I watched the match that I understood what had been in the manager's mind. The Hungarians were 2-0 up in fifteen minutes and playing superbly. It was the best football I have ever seen, brilliant first-time movement. But the pitch was getting heavier and heavier. Honved gradually got bogged down, their tricks got stuck in the mud. Billy Wright and Ron Flowers kept slinging these huge long passes up to the Wolves forwards. The mud just wore the Hungarians out.

"What I also remember is that the noise of the crowd was quite phenomenal, and I don't think I've heard a noise quite like it at a football match in all my time in the game at Manchester United and other clubs, or even working as a TV commentator. It was quite awesome. Another personal memory I have is of the next morning. One of my jobs was to sweep up the great terracing areas and I found a one pound note, which was a fortune to a young lad in those days. I couldn't believe my luck."

Honved were quickly ahead in the match with a goal from

Kocsis, who headed in a free-kick from Puskas, chief orchestrater of the Hungarian footballing rhapsody. Kocsis turned provider for the second, his pass allowing Machos to race through and score.

Half-time brought relief from the bewitching football of the visitors. Like the interval in the FA Cup semi-final against Manchester United in 1949, this must be regarded as one of the most crucial moments for Cullis as a manager. The prospect was of yet another crushing home loss for an English team against Hungarians, and the second half of the match was due to be shown live on television around the country. The Iron Manager knew it was a moment for cool analysis and motivation rather than blind anger.

Cullis focused first on a tactical switch. He had noticed how the Honved full-backs were playing a little square, so he demanded that his players feed wingers Mullen and Hancocks with quickfire passes. He also ordered Bill Slater and Ron Flowers to stop trying to smother Puskas and Kocsis on the ball, a task that was proving impossible, but to to cut off the supply to the world's best footballers instead. Cullis read a game brilliantly, thanks to his own football intuition and countless hours studying the strategies of other teams.

What had he said at half time? He remembered later: "I told them, 'Let's have an all-out effort and use the long ball more. You are trying to carry it too far in the mud'."

Slater also recalled the mood at the interval, saying: "At half-time I do remember Stan being very relaxed about the situation even though we were 2-0 down. I think a few us were expecting one of his dressing-room blasts, but he just went round the players talking quietly about what was needed in the second half. He gave out this air of confidence that we could get back into the match, and so it proved."

The huge crowd at Molineux, and the TV viewers at home, saw the effects almost immediately as a long ball forward brought a penalty four minutes into the second half. Hancocks kept his nerve to score from the spot. The match was alive, and the Wolves players sensed that the recovery Cullis had demanded in the dressing-room was a real possibility.

Geoffrey Green, football correspondent of *The Times*, the doyen of purple prose, captured the mood sitting in the packed press box. "Bit by bit Wolves began to tighten the screws," he wrote. "Their shirts of old-gold, trimmed with black at the edges and specially treated with luminous effect for night matches, began to fill the dark field. They seemed to double in number and swarm everywhere. The pitch, more and more churned up, resembled thick glue. And the Molineux crowd surged, tossed and roared like a hurricane at sea, and called for the kill."

Honved resisted incessant Wolves attacks for nearly thirty minutes more, even though their legs were tiring as heavy rain transformed the pitch into a morass. Eventually the dam broke as Cullis's team scored twice in ninety seconds as time was running out. In the 76th minute Swinbourne headed in a cross from Dennis Wilshaw. Soon after the pair combined again as this time a Wilshaw pass allowed Swinbourne to run on and shoot home the goal that cheered up a whole nation, never mind a town bursting with pride.

At that time TV commentaries were restrained affairs compared to the excitable men behind the microphones now. That night the BBC commentator was beside himself with excitement, shouting after the third goal: "He's scored, he's scored, he's scored, Hancocks has scored." In fact it had been Swinbourne, but no-one was complaining.

Wilshaw had nearly missed the game. He also worked as a teacher in Staffordshire and after school lessons had finished he drove to the game through torrential rain. As he passed over a railway bridge in the town of Stone, a boy pushed his bicycle in front of Wilshaw's car. He hit the brakes, but nothing happened. Luckily, the car struck only the bicycle and the lad was unharmed. A policeman happened to be on the bridge, recognised the famous driver, a player who would later memorably score four goals for England in an international against Scotland, and told Wilshaw: 'Oh it's you, bugger off'.

"It was the best game I ever played for Wolves," said Wilshaw. "Yet in the first half all I had been doing was marvelling at the ability and class of the Honved players."

Goalkeeper Bert Williams summed up his feelings neatly, saying: "That night against Honved must have been one of the ten greatest matches ever played in the history of football."

Millions of radio listeners did miss the final tense moments of this unforgettable match as the BBC faded out commentary ninety seconds from the end of the game and switched to a broadcast of the *Show Band Show*. It provoked a storm of protest as football fans were left wondering whether or not Wolves had won a famous victory. The BBC interrupted the music later to announce the final score, but many had switched off then, and there was no way of learning the score in those days until reading the morning newspaper.

The papers all delivered a stunning story which filled the front pages as well as the back. The most famous headline the next day was in the *Daily Mail*, which used Cullis's own words in the emotion after the game to proclaim, "Hail Wolves, 'Champions of the world'."

Their reporter David Wynne-Morgan wrote: "In the dressing-room afterwards Stanley Cullis, his eyes filled with tears, went up to Billy Wright and said: "Magnificent."

The *Daily Mirror* had dispatched star sports columnist Peter Wilson to Molineux. He was tagged as 'The Man They Can't Gag', a man who made his reputation with tough, vivid journalism and who did not give praise lightly. His verdict was: "I may never live to see a greater thriller than this. And if I see many more as thrilling I may not live much longer anyway."

Charles Buchan, writing in the *News Chronicle*, was overjoyed, and perhaps felt a little vindicated, too, as he said: "Wolves struck another decisive blow for British football with as wonderful a second-half rally as I have seen in forty years."

In the dressing-room after the match Cullis gave his famous speech describing his team as champions of the world. He also said: "I thought I could never be more proud of them than when they beat Spartak, but tonight has surpassed everything. The second half was the greatest performance I have ever seen."

Years later Cullis explained how these floodlit night matches meant most to him as a manager, saying: "It was very nice to win

Cups and the League but, for sheer excitement, they were some way behind my fondest memories. The floodlit matches in the mid-1950s were even better. There was nothing to compare with them. They were the high spot of Wolves' entire history. They were fantastic matches and fantastic occasions. It didn't matter for one moment that the matches were only friendlys, and I became quite adept at speech-making what with all the banquets we had after the games."

The player to whom the victory meant more than anyone was captain Billy Wright, who had also been England skipper in both the heavy international losses to Hungary. This time his team had left Puskas tasting the bitterness of defeat. It wasn't the only thing Puskas tasted that night either. Wright recalled: "My abiding memory from that match is of the banquet after the game – and of Puskas's appetite. It was as big as his capacity for work on the football field. Even at the end of a huge meal Puskas was still going strong. I watched, fascinated, as he ate a dozen biscuits, exactly a dozen, laden with butter and Danish blue cheese. I caught his eye as biscuit followed biscuit, pointed to my waistline and shook my head warningly. Puskas just smiled – and carried on eating."

Slater missed the feast. He explained: "After the game I wasn't feeling too well, and I didn't fancy attending the post-match banquet that was traditional. I mentioned this to Stan and he told me not to bother. In fact he even paid for a taxi to take me home to Birmingham that night. That was the only time it ever happened, and I knew then what we had done was something quite special.

"After that night Puskas became a great friend of Billy Wright. Every time he came to England he would travel up to Wolverhampton to see Billy. There was a special bond between them, and with the Wolves because of the Honved match."

Again the telegrams arrived in sackfuls, from fellow managers like Arthur Rowe at Tottenham to humble fans round the country. The theme was insistent – the Great was back in British football. "To Cullis, Football Club, Wolverhampton. Staff and boys of this school for cripple children offer warm congratulations on the

Wolves magnificent vindication of British skill, character and guts on the football field – Headmaster Chailey Heritage Craft School, Sussex," said one.

"Merry Christmas Wolves and thanks for kicking out the daylight of the continental teams. Carry on the good work – Friend, Luton," said another.

Reaction across Europe to Cullis's bold boast that his Wolves team could now be regarded as champions of the world was rather different.

Willy Meisl, an Austrian who was a noted expert on football matters across the continent, attempted to give a different perspective to the victory. He pointed out that Honved had also lost 3-2 away to Red Star Belgrade a few days earlier; a Red Star team incidentally that were placed only seventh in the Yugoslav League, and a long way behind leaders Partizan. "No-one called Partizan champions of the world," said Meisl with civilised irony. "Dare I also remark in passing that quagmires are not usually considered the best pitches on which world championships ought to be decided, not even neutral quagmires."

Two other floodlight matches were played over the next two nights by top English clubs against distinguished European club teams. The next evening West Ham played a home fixture against AC Milan of Italy. The score was a 6-0 defeat of the Hammers. Then, 48 hours after Wolves' heroics, Chelsea drew 2-2 at home to Voros Lobogo of Hungary. Again, the continentals thought, this put events at Molineux into a more realistic light.

One man who certainly thought so was Gabriel Hanot, a former French international who was now the highly influential editor of *L'Equipe*, the French newspaper devoted entirely to sport. He wrote a sermon on the issue, saying: "We must wait for Wolves to visit Budapest and Moscow before we proclaim their invincibility. And there are other clubs of international prowess, like Milan and Real Madrid. There is a strong case for starting a European Championship of clubs."

This was a vision that Hanot had first floated many years earlier before the war. But it was Cullis's boast which was the spark that had been needed to translate the idea of a European Cup into reality. There was already the smaller Mitropa Cup, which incorporated teams from the middle European nations like Austria and Czechoslovakia, but Hanot was convinced the time was right for a competition to embrace the entire continent.

He produced a blueprint for a European club tournament which was published in *L'Equipe* later that week in direct response to the Wolves-Honved match. The plan was for every nation to nominate one club, ideally their champions, and for matches to be played midweek on a home and away league basis. Reaction across the continent varied, and the most widespread and enthusiastic response was for a cup competition rather than a league format. The next month, in January 1955, the Spanish FA president, Juan Touzon, wrote an open letter to *L'Equipe* backing the plan and saying it has the full support of the Real Madrid club and its chairman Santiago Bernabeu.

Thus, from the proud boast of Stan Cullis in the Molineux dressing-room, did the European Cup quickly take shape. Encouraged by the positive support he had received, Hanot sent out invitations to eighteen hand-picked clubs to take part in a new competition to start in the autumn of 1955. Chelsea, then leading the title race in the 1954-55 Football League season, were the chosen English club rather than Wolves, the reigning Division One champions. That was a controversial choice given the many victories by Cullis's team against foreign visitors and his own enthusiasm for innovation. Whether Wolves would have been invited had they been top of the table at the time we will never know.

There were still hurdles to be overcome. FIFA, football's world governing body, told *L'Equipe* the European Cup would have to be sanctioned by them or the new European soccer organisation, UEFA. It could not be run by a newspaper. Hanot accepted this, but continued to organise meetings of clubs like Real Madrid, AC Milan, Sporting Lisbon and Moscow Dynamo in April and May 1955. The idea had such momentum that initial resistance and scepticism from FIFA and the fledgling UEFA was swept aside. It would start in September, barely nine months after Wolves had recovered so magnificently to beat Honved.

Sadly, Chelsea were pressurised into withdrawing from the

first European Cup by a blinkered Football League. The argument by League president Arthur Drewry was that magnificent occasions and matches like Wolves' midweek European games were having a significantly detrimental effect on Saturday attendances in Division One. "The time has come to give serious consideration to a curtailment of the number of friendly and other matches which clubs are arranging," Drewry told the League's annual meeting. Chelsea chairman Joe Mears, a member of the League management committee, felt obliged to heed the warning.

Everything we know about Stan Cullis suggests he would have insisted that Wolves play in the inaugural European Cup had they been chosen. He, surely, would have been as strong-minded as his great friend Matt Busby was twelve months later when Busby's strength of character ensured that Manchester United accepted their invitation to play in the 1956-57 European Cup as the new champions of England.

Wolves certainly continued to play a series of high-profile matches against continental opposition before they entered the European Cup themselves by right as League champions in 1958. Their prestige friendlies continued at home and away.

Another classic match was against Moscow Dynamo, who had toured England in the aftermath of the war and created a sensation with a combination of their stylish soccer and an air of mystique. Their sad faces and long, drooping shorts made them appear incredibly strange to the enormous crowd which witnessed a 3-3 draw at Stamford Bridge. Their football was outstanding, and other matches brought a 4-3 win against Arsenal and a 10-1 victory over Cardiff City.

Lev Yashin, clad in his famous all black strip, and one of the most celebrated footballers on earth, was the goalkeeper for Dynamo when they played Wolves a decade later. Within fifteen minutes Yashin was picking the ball out of his net after a goal by Bill Slater. Jimmy Mullen scored a second goal in the 49th minute, and although Ilyin pulled one back for the Russians, Wolves held on for victory. Dynamo were incensed that an 'equaliser' headed into the net by Feodosov was ruled offside by referee Arthur Ellis.

Cullis made a return visit to Moscow in August 1955 for

matches against Dynamo and Spartak. Both were lost. Against Dynamo they were 3-0 down at half-time as Yuri Kuznetsov scored twice after Feodosov avenged his Molineux misery with the opening goal. The 'champions of the world' rallied after the break and Dennis Wilshaw scored twice to set up a tight finish. Again, it was an indication of the value Cullis placed on fitness. Roy Peskett wrote in the *Daily Mail*: "If Wolves are not the best team in the world there can be no greater fighters."

Another way of looking at the two Dynamo matches is to consider the 4-4 aggregate scoreline over both games. In modern times it would have given Wolves victory on the away goals rule. Slater recalled: "There were a series of matches against Yashin. What a goalkeeper and what a character he was. It was a privilege to have scored against him."

The most prestigious home and away friendlies were played against Real Madrid, who by then had already won the first two European Cup competitions. In the autumn of 1957 Wolves went to Real's Chamartin Stadium, as it was called then, and emerged with a hugely creditable 2-2 draw. Bobby Mason and Jimmy Mullen scored for Wolves in front of a 110,000 crowd. "The crowd lit candles in mourning for their team as they had never been beaten or drawn at home to foreign opposition," recalled Mason. Wolves might well have won the match with more luck. Their players felt both Madrid's goals were offside, while Norman Deeley hit the bar with a fierce shot in the last few minutes of the game.

Cullis was delighted. He thought Real's peerless inspiration, Alfredo Di Stefano, had the best balance of any footballer in the world. Now would come the second test, facing the continental champions under the Molineux floodlights. Wolves triumphed 3-2 in an epic encounter and, in effect, had won 5-4 on aggregate over two legs against the club which was to win the European Cup five seasons in succession. Even more than the victory against Honved, perhaps, that was the finest single achievement of The Iron Manager's career.

The rewards for the Wolves players in financial terms was paltry. Their win bonus for each of these famous European games was just two pounds, less tax. It was an issue that led to problems at many clubs playing such prestige friendlies in front of capacity 50,000-plus crowds, and which eventually brought the showdown in the early 1960s that ended forever the days of the maximum wage for footballers. One Wolves match against Athletic Bilbao was actually cancelled in a dispute over cash. Players' union leader Jimmy Guthrie, the former Portsmouth captain involved in the shaky signatures episode in the 1939 FA Cup Final lost by Cullis, was leading a nationwide campaign on the issue and travelled to Molineux to lobby the players. Guthrie told the quartet of Billy Wright, Bert Williams, Jesse Pye and Jimmy Mullen they should insist on 'overtime' pay for evening work.

Wolves against Bilbao was the first match in the firing line and the players held a secret ballot on the delicate issue. The vote, by a small margin, was in favour of refusing to play the match, effectively a wildcat strike.

Bill Slater remembered the issue well: "Stan had a problem when there was a call for strike action over the Bilbao match. The PFA had ordered a vote of the players. Stan hated that and called a big meeting to make sure we knew his feelings. The vote was not to play and the match was cancelled. I voted with the PFA line. I didn't feel in my position, earning another salary outside the game at the university, that I could do otherwise."

Cullis, naturally, was furious. He was the manager in charge of the club and it was for him to decide when and against whom his team turned out. Player power, however tentative, would strike at the heart of his authoritarian style of management. He ordered the players to meet with Wolves chairman Joe Baker, who told them he was sympathetic, as Cullis was, to being paid more cash, but that Football League rules expressly forbade it. No compromise was reached and the match was cancelled.

The incident was recalled by Guthrie, who said: "To their everlasting credit the Molineux directors saw the players' point of view and the game was called off. It was said that the ban was enforced because of a personal grudge I held against Wolves, but that was absurd."

Reward for the skill and endeavour of the Wolves players did come in the form of England call-ups, with the Molineux side providing the entire half-back line during the 1958 World Cup where England were the only side which didn't lose to the eventual champions Brazil and their seventeen-year-old prodigy Pele. England boss at the time was Walter Winterbottom, an educated man who had joined the Football Association staff as a result of his wartime army service, becoming director of coaching and eventually England team manager. It was a route Cullis might have taken himself had he not been the England captain and still one of the finest players of the time.

The England call-ups could anger Cullis at times, however, not because he resented his men having time away from the club, but because Winterbottom would ask them to play in different positions than they did for Wolves. Winterbottom recalled: "We used to have arguments sometimes. He had some old-fashioned ideas, one of which was that he didn't believe I should pick players out of their club position when they were turning out for England. A great example was Billy Wright, who had switched positions as his career developed and eventually became a wonderful centre-half with the Wolves. I liked to try out different ideas and on one occasion it seemed to me that it would be useful to have Billy playing at inside right against Austria to mark their best player, Ocwirk. Stan was furious when he found out and got his chairman to create an uproar about the matter. I could see his argument up to a point, and we got on famously really.

"Stan was one of the great managers. He was always thinking about the game, coaching the team, making sure they trained properly. He was one of the first to do that you see. When he started most of them were cheque-book managers who did no coaching at all. With England you could only go for players who were internationally adaptable – and we always looked at Stan's players because they had had success against high-class foreign teams. After the Munich air disaster, I recall, we picked whole of Wolves half-back line for the '58 World Cup."

Wolves finally made it into the European Cup, three years late in the eyes of their fans, in the autumn of 1958 after becoming League champions for the second time. UEFA had wanted to invite Manchester United as well in the wake of the Munich tragedy earlier that year, but the Football League blocked the idea claiming other clubs were against it.

Cullis, a great friend of United's recovering manager Matt Busby, and whose own family prayed every night at home for the lives of Busby and Duncan Edwards, critically injured in the plane crash, ensured that Wolves were not one of those dissenting clubs.

The first round draw paired his team against Schalke 04, the champions of Germany. Wolves were strong favourites, with a clutch of players in their side like Peter Broadbent, Eddie Clamp, Billy Wright and Bill Slater who had played in the 1958 World Cup finals for an England side which had done so well against the brilliant Brazilians. Wolves had to play the first leg at home, and conceded an early goal to centre-forward Siebert and were 1-0 down at half-time, their proud unbeaten home record against continentals under threat. Cullis had been here before, of course, and his half-time sermon brought a whirlwind start to the second half.

"Four minutes after the interval Wolves began one of their great comebacks," wrote Bill Holden in the *Daily Mirror*. "It was power play in the strictest sense from Wolves as they battled for the lead." Broadbent headed an equaliser in the 49th minute and made it 2-1 with another superb header midway through the second half. The Molineux crowd roared its delight – until silenced by an 88th minute goal from Schalke's outside right Koslowski. It was a stunning blow, and Holden added: "Wolves are going to find it mighty tough to survive in the European Cup now."

So it proved in the return leg in Gelsenkirchen a week later. Koerdl put Schalke ahead in the twelfth minute and Siebert added a second to make it 2-0 at half-time. Again, there was a recovery after a dressing-room lecture from Cullis that sparked some ferocious play from Wolves out on the pitch. Young striker Allan Jackson, deputising for the injured Jimmy Murray, scored in the 48th minute to set up a tense finale. "Wolves rugged brand of fighting soccer had the 43,000 German fans yelling and booing in a tough second half," wrote Bill Holden in the Mirror. "Just as in the first leg Wolves dominated a tempestuous, fast-action match, but they only succeeded once in the vital job of getting the ball in the net."

The controversial defeat ruined Cullis's hopes of another crack at Real Madrid later in the competition, and of a chance to participate in a new world club championship that was being mooted. A UEFA official revealed that the South American governing body had suggested a four-team tournament for the summer of 1959 involving the two Finalists of the European Cup and against the pair of clubs who reached the equivalent Libertadores Cup in South America that was just being launched.

"It sounds a good idea," Cullis had told the *Mirror*, ever eager to broaden the frontiers for football in general and Wolves in particular. "But I suppose it will have to considered by the FA first." Real Madrid were Europe's first participants when the World Club Cup did start in 1960.

The setback against Schalke did not shake Cullis's faith in his style of football, even though rapidly improving defensive organisation among European clubs made them less susceptible to being battered into submission by the Wolves tactic of direct long-passing attacks.

He summed up his own feelings this way, saying: "My ambition as a manager was to win the first division championship, not the European Cup. Until I became manager Wolves had never won the League. We won it in 1954, and again four years later, by playing attacking football, which was my whole philosophy. In the late 1950s we scored more than 100 goals for four years in succession. Of course, that made us vulnerable at the back, but that was our style. To win the European Cup required a different style. It required the players to go against their natural game, and this I was not prepared to do."

Given all we know about Cullis, especially the enjoyment he found in pitting his wits against the best continental teams available, this explanation doesn't ring wholly true. It sounds like the kind of public excuse it is sometimes prudent for managers to broadcast to the world. That is not a criticism, merely an observation. Cullis did experiment with tactics within the broad framework of his belief in the long-ball style, and it is hard to believe he would have accepted that his team were doomed to failure in the European Cup.

Back home Wolves romped to the First Division title again in the 1958-59 season. They were undeniably the most powerful team in the land. That success brought a second crack at the European Cup, beginning with another German club, Vorwaerts, based in East Berlin.

Peter Broadbent scored a vital goal in the 2-1 away defeat in the first leg, and Wolves won the return 2-0 with ease thanks to strikes from Broadbent and Bobby Mason.

Football writer Ken Jones, nephew of Bryn Jones, a team-mate of Cullis in the 1930 Wolves team, has a vivid memory of that night. He said: "Stan used to have fierce put-downs for the players to keep them in their place. Half-back Eddie Clamp, an England international, was a truly tough footballer. That night against Vorwaerts he suffered a terrible leg injury and was carried off on a stretcher; he simply couldn't walk. As the stretcher came past the manager's bench Cullis stood up and said with heavy sarcasm to Clamp, 'So you think you're hard then?' That was typical of Stan's style with the players."

The retirement of skipper Billy Wright did not seem to affect the side as Bill Slater was switched to centre-half, with Clamp and Ron Flowers playing at half-back. Next up were Red Star Belgrade, rugged opponents who were held 1-1 in Belgrade in a match scarred by violent play. Threats and counter-threats were made among the players, although an allegation that the Yugoslavs were were warned "to bring your coffins with you" for the second leg is most likely an apocryphal tale. There could be no doubting the emphatic scoreline in the match at Molineux, a 3-0 home victory sealed by Jimmy Murray's early goal and two towards the end from Mason.

At last this seemed to be the real Wolves, back on the glory trail, inspired by the Molineux floodlights. Expectation was high for the quarter-final visit to Barcelona, a team coached by Helenio Herrera, another manager who, like Cullis, was a master of psychology and a keen student of tactics. Herrera pinned slogans all over the dressing-room walls in one ploy to motivate his players, and he would later be credited with developing the infamous 'catenaccio' defensive tactic of Inter Milan in the 1960s, and his Barcelona team were masters of counter-attacking play. The all-out attacking style of Wolves played perfectly into their hands and Barcelona elegantly and clinically destroyed Cullis's team with a 4-0 victory in what was then called the Gran Estadio. The Spanish press were scathing, saying: "Wolves, like all English teams, continue to play football that is twenty years behind the time." Barcelona's goals reflected their cosmopolitan side; two from the Uruguayan winger Villaverde, one from Brazilian striker Evaristo and a fourth scored by Ladislav Kubala, a Hungarian who became a naturalised Spaniard.

There was a three-week wait for the return leg at Molineux. No-one really believed that Wolves could overturn a four-goal deficit, but there was honour at stake, and of course their proud unbeaten home record. Bill Slater had missed the first leg, as he did many European away matches, because he could not get time off from his job as a lecturer. Slater was welcomed back for the game at Molineux, while Barcelona also made a change, introducing Sandor Kocsis into their attack in place of Kubala. This was the same Kocsis who had scored for Honved in their 3-2 defeat six years earlier – and he returned to the Black Country with a vengeance, scoring four goals himself as Barcelona won 5-2 for a crushing 9-2 aggregate victory.

The pitch that night in March 1960 was muddy, the rain was pelting down, and a noisy capacity crowd seemed to make the occasion a replica of the atmosphere against Honved. But European football had moved on, standards raised immensely both by the competitive edge the club tournament provided and by the vast new incomes it generated. Cullis's holy trinity was still in place – team spirit, supreme fitness, and efficient tactics. But a fourth element was needed now to compete at the highest level – and that was world-class talent with a football at a player's feet.

Wolves fought gallantly against Barcelona, Murray and Mason both on the scoresheet. But there was no answer to the artistry and deadly finishing of Kocsis. Villaverde added the other goal which gave Barcelona a semi-final showdown against Real Madrid. Cullis was generous in his praise to opponents who had given Wolves a harsh lesson in the new realities of modern football.

Slater recalled: "The Barcelona game stands out for me among the European Cup games. We had lost so heavily in the away match that we had to attack for goals at home. It made us vulnerable to the great players they possessed in their team. I think that does much to explain the scoreline that night."

Cullis himself was philosophical. There was not point in being angry.

"If we had to be beaten, I'm glad it was by a team like this," said the Iron Manager.

If rusty strategy was undermining his team in Europe, it certainly didn't show at home in England. Wolves won the FA Cup in 1960 and missed out on the first Double of League and Cup in the 20th century by a single point as Burnley snatched the title.

Barcelona themselves lost 3-1 in both the home and away legs of their European Cup semi-final against Real Madrid, bringing the sack for Herrera and taking Real to the greatest of all the Finals, the 7-3 victory against Eintracht Frankfurt in May 1960. Di Stefano scored a hat-trick in the Final at Hampden Park, while Ferenc Puskas, showing no ill effects from his passion for blue cheese and biscuits, trumped that with four goals.

It gave Real Madrid a fifth successive European Cup title since the tournament had been launched as a consequence of Wolves beating Honved and Puskas 3-2 one rainy December night at Molineux. How fitting it should be that Stan Cullis was among the incredulous 130,000 crowd at Hampden watching Puskas in action again to see the magnificent consequence of the bold declaration that his team were 'champions of the world'.

Chapter Eight

Kings of England

"...When they call me a genius, they little realise how near it is to calling me a fool..." Stan Cullis

THROUGH eleven years of entertaining, fast and skilful football from 1949 to 1960 Wolves won the FA Cup twice and the Football League title three times; and we have already seen their long-lasting impact on the European game. The only club that matched them was Matt Busby's Manchester United. That team, and Busby himself, are revered in English football history. Cullis and the Wolves are mostly treated as a footnote in comparison, and this is a fact which rankles, understandably, with those closely involved with the club at the time, from England international and Cup Final captain Bill Slater to groundstaff boy Ron Atkinson.

"Stan never received the accolades he deserved," said Slater. "I don't know whether he was offered recognition and turned it down on principle, but I do believe it was very wrong that he wasn't more widely acknowledged for his success. He was a wonderful manager who deserves to be placed among the very best."

There is no record of Stan Cullis receiving such an offer.

Atkinson, who later managed clubs like Manchester United, Aston Villa and Atletico Madrid, added: "Stan is a legend of football and it is disgraceful that his achievements have largely been forgotten. Wolves and Manchester United were the two clubs of the 1950s and Stan built the team at Molineux. Brian Clough and Alex Ferguson have a reputation for ruling their clubs with an iron fist. But make no mistake, no-one ever had more authority at his club than Stan Cullis. And when you bear in mind that his side was full of top-class international players that was no mean achievement.

"He and Matt Busby vied as the managerial giants of the 1950s. Everyone knows about the Busby Babes. Wolves had the Cullis Cubs, and they won almost every FA Youth Cup between them during that decade. It is very sad that he didn't get the recognition he deserved."

Cullis's first season as manager at Molineux would alone have ensured his reputation. He took charge at the age of 31 and led his team to sixth place in the League and victory in the Cup Final at Wembley. They beat Chesterfield, Sheffield United, Liverpool and Black Country rivals West Brom on the way, but the crucial tie was a dramatic semi-final against Busby's Manchester United, the Cup holders.

The match was staged at Hillsborough, and Wolves began with problems because their influential centre-forward Jesse Pye had barely recovered from a major bout of 'flu. Six minutes into the match the left-back, Roy Pritchard, was badly hurt and, before the days of substitutes, was compelled to play as a passenger on the left wing. Right back Laurie Kelly was later carried off on a stretcher after another serious knock. Captain Billy Wright recalled the "unworldly tension" of the half-time interval where one word out of place might have destroyed the team's morale. Instead, Stan Cullis was a master of the situation, quietly bolstering the confidence of his ravaged team. At times like this he would go round the dressing-room having a few words with each player. In the second half Wolves responded with pride and gallantry, courageously withstanding an onslaught of United attacks; what football people like to call an Alamo match.

The replay was at Goodison, the ground where Cullis had received two of his worrying head injuries, and not far from the family home in Ellesmere Port. It was a significant venue for a crucial match of his managerial career. The team had to be patched up because both regular full-backs were out injured from the first game. In came reserve left-back Terry Springthorpe, and on the other side was Alf Crook, normally a right-half in the reserves. For this match Cullis fired up the Wolves side with a passionate team talk that was reflected in some fierce tackling by Springthorpe on United's dangerous winger Jimmy Delaney.

Busby, as we know, was the closest of personal friends with Cullis, but that afternoon he was sent into a rage on the trainer's bench and the two men shared angry opinions as the whirlwind of action played out in front of them. "If only I'd had a recorder with me," said Cullis's assistant Joe Gardiner later. It would have been a collector's item. Wolves won the replay 2-1, displaying all the resilience, fitness and team spirit that would be the hallmark of Cullis teams. And what a start for the young manager – a Cup Final in his first season.

The Final was at Wembley against Leicester City, a side struggling to escape relegation to the third division that season, and selection for the match brought another dilemma for the fledgling boss. Should he restore fit-again full-back Lol Kelly or keep faith with the heroes of the semi-final? Billy Wright remembered that well, saying: "We set off on the Thursday for the Final and I asked Stan Cullis early in the journey what the team would be. After Kelly, who had played at right-back for most of the season, found out he wasn't in the side he got off the coach at Oxford. He was that upset and disappointed; it absolutely broke his heart. Stan threatened him with all sorts of consequences but the matter was never mentioned again. I think the manager put himself in Lol's shoes when he had calmed down and realised how he would have reacted."

Wolves were overwhelming favourites, just as they had been in 1939 against Portsmouth when Cullis was captain of a team which played nervously and lost surprisingly. This time there were no mistakes in a side that included skipper Wright, goalkeeper Bert Williams, half-back Bill Shorthouse and wingers Jimmy Mullen and Johnny Hancocks. Centre-forward Jesse Pye scored twice in the first half to put Wolves in command of the game. After half-time, though Welsh international Mel Griffiths pulled a goal back for second division underdogs Leicester, who then also had a second effort disallowed for offside. It took a superb third strike from Irish international inside-forward Sammy Smyth to ensure a 3-1 final scoreline. The young Wolves manager instinctively played out the match on the Wembley benches, three times knocking his assistant Joe Gardiner clean off his seat.

Cullis later said he was "very satisfied" with his first season as a manager. He was never a man to waste words.

The Wembley victory gave Wolves their first trophy since lifting the FA Cup in 1908. The celebrations were sustained, and for the new manager there was a huge welling of emotion as he took the FA Cup back to the Cullis household in Oldfields Road, Ellesmere Port to show his ageing father Billy, the 'Waffler' from Wolverhampton. There was also a special dinner held in Blackpool at a fine hotel in the seaside town.

Stan's daughter Susan tells the story. She said: "My father could be very eccentric and forgetful, especially away from the world of football, almost as if it was then that he could relax and switch his mind off. They went to Blackpool for this FA Cup party and he was dancing with my mother in the ballroom, they loved dancing, when one of the hotel staff came and gently tapped him on the shoulder. My father was asked whether they were staying in a certain room and when he said 'yes', he was shown an area on the ceiling where water was dripping down into the ballroom. My father had put the bath on but then forgotten about it, perhaps taking a phone call from someone, and then come down without realising the water was still running!"

The next season Wolves were again a whisker away from winning the League Championship for the first time in their history since they began life as the St Luke's College football team in the 1870s. Twelve matches without defeat gave Cullis's men a hurricane start to the 1949-50 season. From the first week in October until Boxing Day, however, they didn't win a single game. It coincided with the double blow of losing goalkeeper Williams and skipper Wright, who had both been injured playing for England against Wales; club versus country conflicts are nothing new in the game. Another problem lay at centre-forward, where even an enthusiastic full-back, Angus McLean, was tried once and responded with a goal against Portsmouth at Molineux.

In the New Year results improved and Wolves were involved in a thrilling battle with Portsmouth for the title. The sides eventually ended level on 53 points from 42 games in a season where no team stood out. Portsmouth, indeed, managed to take the championship despite losing eleven matches. Wolves finished with four wins and a draw from their last five games and beat Birmingham 6-1 at Molineux on the final day, with winger Johnny Hancocks even missing a penalty. But Portsmouth also won 5-1 against Aston Villa the same day and took the title on goal average. As the *Express and Star* reporter said: "As things turned out Wolves needed to win 20-1 on the final day."

Throughout this time Cullis knew the team had to be improved. His first and most important source of new players was an innovative youth policy. He had tens of thousands of boys watched by hundreds of scouts all round the country, many of them unpaid, like his own brothers Billy and Sydney in Ellesmere Port. They were co-ordinated by George Noakes, a former steel mill worker who joined Wolves full-time during the war. Cullis trusted his judgement implicitly and signed many youngsters on the say-so of Noakes.

One of those youngsters was Ron Atkinson, who recalled: "I was playing Midlands county football and was spotted by George Noakes, the legendary Wolves scout who only had one eye. I went into their youth training system after an interview with Mr Cullis. I can't really recall what he said but you knew he had a tremendous presence as a man. I was approached by several clubs at the time, but Wolves were the top team then and there was no choice at all in my mind."

Apart from nationwide scouting system Cullis was also the first to develop a nursery club. This was Wath Wanderers, based at

Wath-on-Dearne near Barnsley, set up and run by a former Wolves team-mate of Cullis in the 1930s, Mark Crook. After retiring as a lively winger Crook bought a fish shop in Yorkshire and wanted to help youngsters with talent. Many sportsmen went through the Wath system, including the Robledo brothers who played for Newcastle in the 1950s and England cricketer Johnny Wardle, who had trials as a footballer at Molineux.

The most famous pair of players from this soccer nursery were Ron Flowers and Roy Swinbourne, who both won England caps. They were called the two 'Grapes of Wath' by an inspired headline writer. Swinbourne made an impressive start to his career in that 1949-50 season, and was among the first of a new generation of players that Cullis introduced to transform the team from nearly-men in the League to triple champions.

A newcomer in 1951 was the brilliant inside-forward Peter Broadbent, signed from Brentford. Cullis called that the best buy he ever made. Others to arrive included Norman Deeley and half-back Bill Slater, who had played for the England amateur side in the 1952 Olympics and as an amateur in the 1951 FA Cup Final for Blackpool. Gradually, the team was moulded into the fighting unit that Cullis desired, with every player committed to giving 100 per cent.

Slater remembers well his interview with Cullis. He had been offered a job as a lecturer at Birmingham University and wanted to play in the Midlands. Cullis knew he was a good player, but wondered about the academic man's attitude.

"I was perhaps a little nervous on that first meeting and mumbled something about not minding which team I played in," said Slater. "Given that I was working as a lecturer and could only train part-time I thought that was a reasonable thing to say. Stan looked at me hard and told me, 'If you don't want to play in the first team you're no good to us.' Of course I was desperate to play in the first team at the Wolves, and I said that was exactly what I wanted to do. Thankfully, he took me on."

Cullis demanded 100 per cent commitment in every game. Players he felt were slacking soon found themselves transferred, even talented men like Sammy Smyth, who left for Stoke City. The change in personnel was gradual; evolution rather than revolution, which is the mark of an intelligent manager. Wholesale clear-outs rarely succeed in football.

Chief scout Noakes and manager Cullis refused to make illegal payments to promising youngsters as a matter of principle, even though it meant missing out on boys they were keen to sign. But they were not averse to sharp practice, like giving rival scouts wrong directions to a talented lad's house while they signed him up. "All's fair in love and football scouting," Cullis once said. He used to chuckle, too, at the memory of one incident when a scout asked for danger money in trying to sign up a boy because there was a fierce dog at his house. The Iron Manager refused to pay up and wrote a letter himself to the youngster. Three days later it was returned undelivered by the Post Office with an accompanying note: 'Dog at Large'.

Another method of improvement that Cullis strongly believed in was regular trips to sunny climates. After Wolves had finished in a disappointing fourteenth place in the 1950-51 season, although they did reach the semi-finals of the FA Cup losing 2-1 to Newcastle in a replay, he took them on a seven-week summer tour of South Africa. His philosophy was explained in *All For The Wolves*, where he wrote: "Warm sunshine beating down on the backs of athletes helps to build a suppleness of muscle which can never be achieved completely in colder climates. Whatever changes are made to English football, even playing through the summer, we must not expect our footballers to match the finesse and ball-artistry of the brilliant Brazilians. They have the advantages of sunshine which no amount of money or ingenuity can bring to England."

Friendly journalists like Bob Ferrier of the *Daily Mirror* purveyed the message of Professor Cullis and his scientific approach to the game.

"At the end of last season the Wolves players were sated with football," wrote Ferrier in a preview to the 1951-52 season. "The tour of South Africa, where there was abundant food and sunshine, should have refreshed the players."

Stan Cullis kept mementoes and accounts of the tour in his private collection. On the official brochure he has written in all the teams and scorers. One reason, surely, is that it was on this tour that he scored his one and only goal in the colours of Wolver-hampton Wanderers.

The side won all twelve of the matches they played from 12 May to 3 July 1951, including two 'Test' matches against the South African national side. The least demanding of the fixtures was at Mossel Bay against a timid South Western Districts team, and 34-year-old Cullis, enjoying the sunshine, fancied a game, no doubt hoping to show the younger professionals on the trip what a good player he could still be. The match was an 11-0 walkover and the manager who kicked every ball of every match on the sidelines was overjoyed to have scored a goal himself, something he never achieved in his First Division and international career. He had also performed exceptionally well.

"Ha," he snorted at the end of ninety minutes. "I can still show these youngsters a thing or two about playing this game."

Later in the tour at East London this success persuaded him to have another go in the side, especially as the squad had a couple of injuries and some players needed a rest. This time, however, the opposition was far tougher. Cullis, his match fitness, if not his footballing prowess, long gone, was run into the ground. Characteristically, he refused to leave the field, and was in physical distress for days afterwards, to the amusement and respect of the players. It was a mistake he did not repeat. Managers cannot parade their indignity too often.

Sunshine on their backs did not bring immediate reward. In the following season, despite Ferrier's optimism, Wolves lang-uished in sixteenth position, their worst since promotion in the early 1930s. Cullis would have argued for the long-term benefit of the trip, and in the subsequent nine seasons Wolves finished in the top three eight times. The odd season they finished 'only' sixth.

A subsequent visit to South Africa in the summer of 1957 presaged the winning of the title in the following League campaign. Again, they had a 100 per cent tour record, winning eight matches out of eight, including South Africa 4-1 and Northern Rhodesia 11-1.

The visit was most memorable, however, for the day Cullis was sent off on the touchline for his furious response to a refereeing decision. Even in such relatively undemanding fixtures the obsession still took complete hold of his personality when a match was in progress. Norman Deeley was beside Cullis on the sidelines that hot afternoon and recalled the incident with amusement, saying: "Once he took off his hat and threw it on the ground, stamped on it. There was an enclosure with about 20,000 fans behind. They were having a go at him, so about five minutes from the end he took his hat off and said: 'Hold that Norman'. I held his hat, then he took off his watch and said: 'Hold that'. And I said: 'What are you doing?' And he said: 'I think we're going to be in a fight'. I thought: 'twenty-thousand against us and he's ready to have a fight!'"

The 1952-53 season provided vindication of the thorough methods of Cullis. In the League Wolves finished a creditable third, just three points behind champions Arsenal. The reserve team won the Central League for the third year in succession, the best evidence yet of the strength in depth at the club which Cullis knew to be essential for long-term success. The youth team, including a teenage Eddie Clamp, reached the first-ever Final of the FA Youth Cup, losing 9-3 on aggregate over two legs to Manchester United.

Twelve months later the Busby Babes and the Cullis Cubs met again in the Final of the FA Youth Cup. A crowd of 18,000 watched the first match at Old Trafford, a thrilling 4-4 draw. Around 28,000 fans went to Molineux for the second leg where United won 1-0 to take the trophy. The pride of the two great managerial pals can be imagined.

Ron Atkinson remembers those days well, saying: "There was so much competition at Wolves that I was lucky to get into the fourth team. So my father thought I would do better to take an apprenticeship in engineering and perhaps try my luck at another club like Aston Villa. There was a schemozzle about that and Stan did try to persuade me to stay at Molineux. At the Villa it wasn't too long before I became a regular reserve team player. That was the difference with Wolves then.

"Stan always gave you impression that while he was hard he was also a totally fair man. You could go and talk to him at any time. But as apprentices when we even heard him walking along the corridor we would hide just in case we were on the end of a thick ear for something or other. Sometimes we'd be sweeping up the corridor walking behind him thinking that. But I do remember that he was always very fair with the youngsters when they had the menial jobs to do."

By the summer of 1953 Cullis had built what many considered was his greatest side. Bert Williams was in goal, South African Eddie Stuart was at full-back. The half-back line included Bill Shorthouse, Billy Wright and Bill Slater, with Ron Flowers available too. In attack Jimmy Mullen and Johnny Hancocks were at the peak of their powers as wingers, while Peter Broadbent and Dennis Wilshaw were talented inside-forwards. At centre-forward was Roy Swinbourne, who couldn't stop scoring. In fact, the whole team couldn't, netting 96 goals in the season as Wolves finally clinched their first championship. Mullen and Hancocks scored 31 goals between them, and the *FA Year Book* said of them: "Probably no two wingers have been closer in touch with the other during a game than this pair. Their wing-to-wing movements, combined with long diagonal passes that change the point of attack, throughout constituted a dangerous threat to opponents."

The season began, as many Cullis seasons did, in emphatic manner. They went unbeaten from 29 August to 12 December. With Stan Cullis in charge you were not allowed to begin a season half-heartedly. Three crucial away victories seemed to mark this out as a special season. Wolves won at Newcastle for the first time in fifty years, at Arsenal for the first time in 21 years, and away at local rivals West Bromwich Albion for the first time in nineteen years. Most significant of all was that match at The Hawthorns. Albion were the closest pursuers of Cullis's team that season, and eventually finished four points adrift. If West Brom had won at home against Wolves, the clubs would have been level on points. As it was, the other Black Country side had to be content with winning the FA Cup Final.

The League title was decided and on the last day of the season, as Bill Slater recalled: "We beat Spurs, and West Brom lost on the same day, 3-0 at Portsmouth. We all knew that had settled it."

After the Honved match this must have been Cullis's second finest moment. He had come so close to winning the title before the war as a young captain. He had pulled out of that tackle with Albert Stubbins in the final match of his career in 1947, refusing to contemplate victory with a professional foul. In his second season as a manager the title had been lost on the narrow margin of goal difference. Now his father's home town had the glory of winning the League Championship at last.

If Cullis was exultant it didn't register with players like Slater. He said: "There was no great emotion from Stan. He was so focused on the job he was doing for that kind of personal stuff to show in public. Stan was a very private man in many ways. We knew little about him as a person, aside from the fact that he was a strong churchgoer."

Here was a man at the height of his fame, the match against Honved played a few months after this first Championship triumph. But Stan Cullis did not actively seek the limelight. If it helped the Wolves cause to talk in public he would do so, and after matches he could rarely stop himself sometimes. Otherwise, his privacy was sacrosanct – although this did lead to occasional problems.

At around this time the Cullis family moved home between two houses just 100 yards apart on the same street in the Tettenhall area of Wolverhampton. Despite being a relatively affluent and famous man, he decided he would personally undertake as much of the removals work as he could himself, carrying his furniture along the pavement. A policeman thought it looked suspicious when he saw this balding figure struggling along with a fancy armchair and apprehended him.

"My father explained what he was doing and said he was Stan Cullis," said son Andrew. "But the policeman wasn't going to be taken for an idiot and refused to believe him. Dad had to knock on a neighbour's door and ask the man to vouch for him to save being arrested. He wasn't very happy at all about that, just as it used to annoy him terribly when people thought he must swear like a trooper because of the way he approached managing a football team. He never did."

The injustice rankled, as it did with petty fines that he and Wolves suffered for minor incidents from an officious Football Association. There was a £50 punishment for coaching on the bench during an FA Cup tie at Grimsby in January 1955. Wolves eventually lost to Sunderland in the quarter-finals that season. Another case involved an alleged illegal approach in 1959 to a Manchester boy while he was still at school. Cullis was furious that the club was fined £250 over a "frivolous" case that was based on hearsay evidence.

Stan Cullis was a puritanical man in many ways, but that did not prevent what he considered acceptable gamesmanship like the order to Ron Atkinson and the groundstaff boys to water the Molineux pitch further on a day of heavy rain. Ron Greenwood, an innovative manager with West Ham and England, reckoned another trick that Cullis used was "to soak the ball in water before a game."

Wolves were also regularly accused of rough play. After a particularly bitter game against Arsenal in which the Gunners were thrashed 6-1, the opposition manager George Swindin moaned to the press: "We were powered out of the game." Cullis was provoked into an angry response, saying: "It's nonsense to suggest that. They were footballed out of it."

Bill Slater also strongly defends the Wolves side from accusations that they were too vigorous, and from any notion that the Iron Manager ordered them to play dirty. He said: "There is no doubt Wolves were a hard team then; they had that reputation before I joined them. I had been at Blackpool at the start of my career and it was always an occasion when the Wolves came. The mood was that it would be a tough game.

"When I joined them we certainly weren't a dirty team although there were one or two like Eddie Clamp who weren't averse to tough tackles when they were required. We were also such a fit team. Pre-season training was a torture running up and down those hills. But it certainly played a vital part in the success of the team. There wasn't a fitter team anywhere and that helped us in the last few minutes of many matches when the opposition were exhausted. I thank that is an important distinction. We could stay physically strong throughout ninety minutes."

Having won the title, the next question was whether Wolves could retain it? It is a rare feat. During the last fifty years only three clubs have managed it – Wolves later in the 1950s, Liverpool twice in the late 1970s and early 1980s, and Manchester United once in the 1950s and three times in the 1990s. It is another measure of the Cullis success, although the first time they tried to defend the Championship crown his Wolves team managed only second place.

In that 1954-55 season they were again top scorers in the League with 89 goals, but finished four points adrift of champions Chelsea. With the benefit of hindsight there is always a key fixture, and in this campaign it was surely Chelsea's dramatic 1-0 victory at home to Wolves in front of a 75,000 crowd at Stamford Bridge when the gates were closed to a packed house 45 minutes before kick off. Many thousands had to be locked out.

Goalkeeper Bert Williams had a magnificent match, but after 75 minutes was beaten by a powerful shot by Chelsea's Seamus O'Connell. Behind him, however, a wonderful flying leap saw the ball tipped away round the post and the referee, believing it to be another incredible save by the Wolves keeper, gave a corner. Chelsea players protested furiously and the linesman backed up the undisputable fact that the 'save' had in fact been made illegally by centre-half Billy Wright, the England captain. Nowadays, Wright would have been sent off. Then it merely brought a penalty for Chelsea which Peter Sillett converted for the victory that decided the destiny of the title.

The following season, 1955-56, Wolves were the leading goalscorers in the First Division for the third season running. Whatever people made of Stan Cullis's tactics, there was no denying their efficiency. In Cullis's view goals equalled entertainment. Their campaign, however, was undoubtedly hit hard by a bad injury to prolific striker Roy Swinbourne which effectively ended his career. Swinbourne had scored seventeen goals in eleven games in a typically excellent start to the season by Wolves. They could not, however, quite match Matt Busby's Manchester United for sheer class. This was the year when the Busby Babes of the Youth Cup became brilliant senior professionals and won the first of two consecutive titles before the Munich air crash in February 1958.

Wolves finished third, with Blackpool in second place. England and Blackpool full-back Jimmy Armfield remembers facing Cullis's team that season, saying: "Wolves were a strong team, a hard team, and very difficult to beat, so strong running. The biggest gate we had at Blackpool was against Wolves. I remember people sitting on the track at Bloomfield Road with 38,000 inside the ground. Blackpool were second and Wolves top, and we won 2-1. It was Blackpool's best ever League season; we eventually finished second behind Manchester United. Wolves were third.

"I also remember the very first time I played at Molineux, a Saturday sometime in the mid-50s. I had gone down with our manager Joe Smith, who wanted to go and see Stan, who had been a playing contemporary of his. Joe was still upset that Wolves had taken on centre-half Bill Slater, who had been a fine amateur player with Blackpool. I remember walking along the corridor to the manager's office. There were three steps up to it, and a chair just outside. Joe told me to sit on the chair while he went in to see Stan. At that time I was playing for Young England and I did look young. Suddenly, Stan Cullis appeared and said to me 'right son, come in here and we'll talk'. So I went in and when Stan saw Joe he said to him in his usual accent, 'Just give us a minute with this lad'.

"'Oh no you don't,' said Joe. 'He's one of mine and you've already pinched our centre-half.' They had a good chuckle about that.

"I remember the match vividly too. That day Cullis played Billy Wright at left-back to stop Stan Matthews. We won 5-2 at Molineux, and it proved that it was foolish to give Matthews a bit of bait."

At the end of the 1955-56 season came another hint of health problems from Cullis's unquenchable desire for success. He had worked himself to the brink of exhaustion and was ordered by his doctor to take a month's rest during the summer.

Another transition of the side also had to occur around this time, as Swinbourne retired and the veterans Bill Shorthouse and

Bert Williams would retire at the end of 1956-57 after long service at Molineux while Dennis Wilshaw would be transferred to Stoke City in December 1957, to be closer to his teaching job. Replacing them, particularly Swinbourne and Wilshaw in attack, was far from easy. Cullis spent a then club record £20,000 on signing Harry Hooper from West Ham, but it was a move that didn't work and he was fairly quickly shipped out to Birmingham City. In attack the replacements who prospered most were the home-grown talent of Norman Deeley and Jimmy Murray. The 1956-57 season was a period of marking time and regrouping. Wolves finished sixth in the table, and lost 1-0 at home to lowly Bournemouth in the fourth round of the FA Cup. The shock of the result was overshadowed by the fact that one of the goalposts collapsed during the game.

Through all this time, of course, the new recruits and the promoted youngsters were put under the Cullis microscope and through his mental toughening up process. BBC football correspondent Bryon Butler explained: "Stan was a master of tension. That was at the heart of his philosophy as a manager, creating tension and using it to best advantage."

His put-downs to the players were a legend within the dressing-room. If the side were 3-0 ahead at half-time he would tell the players during the interval that the score really ought to be 6-0. He was, on principle, almost never satisfied with a performance. There could always be an improvement somewhere in the team. Roy Swinbourne's purple patch of seventeen goals in eleven games, mentioned earlier, brought a typical Cullis query to the striker.

"How old are you," he asked Swinbourne, who replied with pride that he was just 26 years of age. "I'd better be looking for a replacement then," said Cullis in a gruff voice. He was forever fighting one of football's greatest sins, that of complacency. Every player's attitude was kept firmly in check by the Iron Manager.

Swinbourne explained his feelings about the Cullis methods, saying: "He was hard and wanted the best for the club. We had to toe the line and we had to perform. It was like the sergeant major in the army."

Bill Slater echoed this theme with his own recollections of the way Cullis proved a master of the psychological game between player and manager, much in the way Brian Clough would in later years during his success at Derby County and Nottingham Forest.

"Stan never let up on us," said Slater. "I vividly remember a time when we beat Leeds 3-0. On the Monday he had us in for an hour, talking through all the things we had done wrong before someone finally summoned up the courage to remind him that we had won the match by a convincing scoreline. In one of my first games we beat Cardiff 9-1, and I came into the dressing-room expecting there to be congratulations all round from the manager. Instead, he was picking holes in our performance, making sure we kept our feet on the ground.

"He never swore, though, however angry he might be at a particular moment. And that atmosphere pervaded the dressing-room. I don't think I ever heard a Wolves player swear, certainly not when Stan was around. There was a kind of standard set. He was so honest and so principled, and he demanded loyalty and honesty of effort from his players. If he received it he would back you all the way. If he didn't then a player would soon be out of Molineux."

Talking to football men about Stan Cullis throws up so much affection and humour. Two stories in particular are told with relish about how he dealt with players. One concerns the evening he took a player back on to the pitch after a game had finished. The ground was in darkness, but Cullis lead the poor lad all over the pitch saying to him scathingly, 'now show me where this hole is that you've been hiding in all afternoon'.

TV commentator Kenneth Wolstenholme tells the most famous of all the stories about the Cullis psychology. "There was a day when Wolves had played very badly and in the dressing-room he was very angry and critical of the team, starting with the goalkeeper and going individually through the players right to the number eleven," said Wolstenholme. "After a while he saw one of the reserves smiling, and he then launched into the hapless lad, saying: 'What do you think you've got to laugh about – you not even good enough to get into this team!'"

In the summer of 1957 Cullis took his men to South Africa for another dose of sunshine, and it turned out to be the prelude to three years of magnificent success in domestic football. In the 1957-58 season Wolves won the title again, finishing five points ahead of second-placed Preston North End. They scored 103 goals in the campaign, the first of four consecutive seasons in which they topped the century mark. Cullis was particularly proud of the high skill levels of the forward line he had cultivated at this time. It comprised Deeley, Broadbent, Murray, Mason and Mullen. Cullis said: "Each had considerable style and a forward line such as this, all ball players, hardly justifies the tag of 'kick and rush'. In other clubs all five might have developed into artists of great individuality. At Molineux, however, the individual is primarily a part of the whole and must become units in the team rather than outstanding personages in their own right."

He didn't say so, but Cullis might have been thinking of a contrast with Tom Finney, who was the undoubted star of second-placed Preston; a player for whom we know the Iron Manager had the highest personal regard since picking him as a teenager for his Army XI during the war.

Wolves also won the FA Youth Cup that season, as well as the Central League and Birmingham Combination. It ended Manchester United and Busby's five-year domination of the Youth Cup since its inception. John Giles, a Busby Babe, recalled: "Both clubs made a point of trying to produce home-grown talent and I remember we lost in the semi-final of the Youth Cup that season to Wolves. At every level of the game these were the two great clubs of the time."

This time, too, Wolves completed the task of retaining the League title, which history proves to be so difficult. In the 1958-59 season they ended up six points clear of Busby's Manchester United and netted an incredible 110 goals in the process, with Jimmy Murray again their leading marksman. Sportswriter David Miller remembers covering matches that season for *The Times*, and said: "My recollection is of a series of tough 1-0 victories. They were hard and efficient and gave nothing away. You might say that Stan was the equivalent of an English Bill Shankly in his approach. Much of his team's achievement seemed to me to come through sheer willpower. Stan bestrode the game, he was a very big man and I think it is fair to say that he was held in awe within the game in a variety of ways. It wasn't so much that the players were afraid of him, more that they were afraid of not pleasing him."

In both title-winning seasons Wolves were knocked out of the FA Cup by Bolton Wanderers, who went on to to triumph at Wembley in 1958 after a 2-1 quarter-final victory against Cullis's team.

Cullis was at the height of his power and totally absorbed in his work. His son Andrew recalls the period clearly, remembering how little his father was at home and how privileged he felt to accompany his dad on scouting trips to other matches if he was watching a particular player or studying the tactics of an opposition team. Andrew said: "Our home lives were dominated by football. He was so single-minded about the game, forever thinking about ways he could improve the Wolves team.

"It led to some funny moments too. I remember he took me on a trip to a match at Blackburn, where he wanted to watch a particular player. I was sat in the tea-room with a lemonade while he, as was his wont, talked football in the boardroom. I waited there three hours, having learned to be patient on previous visits to grounds with him. This time he completely forgot I was there and began to drive home alone, reaching the edge of Blackburn before thinking that something wasn't quite right and realising he'd left me at the ground. The ground was empty by then, except for the secretary's wife who had stayed behind to make sure I was all right."

Cullis loved talking football; anywhere and everywhere. And when you are at top of your profession, as he was then, they all listened; directors, players and reporters. Commentator Bryon Butler said: "Stan got very excited after games and would want to talk to half a dozen different people at once about half a dozen different subjects. It was a fascinating spectacle."

Butler also believes that Cullis's continuing concern about the perception of his team as a rather simplistic long-ball side was unnecessary. He added: "Wolverhampton was very tribal in its football. It wasn't the prettiest town in the world, but by golly it had a wonderful football team. It was a case of us against the world. But people didn't have a cordial dislike of the Wolves because of their playing style. The purists crusade against the long-ball wasn't an issue then. It was just because they were the team of the moment, like Arsenal in the 1930s or Manchester United in the present day."

Half-back Bill Slater has a similar outlook about those two back-to-back championship seasons which brought such pride to the town. Slater said: "The talk about our style of football was over-played. I think Stan liked to play up to it himself with the press. We had extremely skilful players like Peter Broadbent and he displayed his talent on the ball. It was direct and fast football, but the passing was accurate not aimless."

When Billy Wright retired at the end of the 1959 season, he was replaced as skipper by Slater. It was perhaps the most dramatic season in the career of Stan Cullis, and he had endured and enjoyed more than his fair share of incredible dramas.

To the very last day of the campaign, Cullis's team chased the Double of League championship and FA Cup in the same season which had eluded every great side for the previous sixty years of the 20th century.

It came to a climax over five days in May 1960. They played against Blackburn Rovers in the Cup Final at Wembley on Saturday, 7 May, having waited in agony the previous Monday to see whether Burnley would pip them in the League by winning their final match away at Manchester City. Wolves had scored 106 goals in reaching 54 points to be top of the table ahead of Burnley, who had their last fixture still to play. Wolves had won 5-1 away at Stamford Bridge in their final match of the League season, but knew a surprise 3-1 home defeat to Spurs in April had given Burnley an opportunity to snatch the title.

The hopes of completing an historic Double lay out of Cullis's hands. His fate lay with the Manchester City side playing at home to Burnley. How Cullis must have wanted to march into the City dressing-room and motivate their players. He had banned his own team from attending the game, arguing that they had to concentrate their minds on the Cup Final to be played a few days later. But he had to be at Maine Road to watch the match in person; it would have been a crowning glory to his managerial reputation.

Journalist David Miller was at the match and remembers it clearly. He said: "My vivid memory of Stan Cullis is seeing him sitting in the front row of the directors' box. He sat there looking as hard as a set of buffers in a railway station, stoney-faced, but otherwise expressionless as he watched his hopes of a third successive League title and the first Double of the 20th century slip away. You could sense the scorn in his whole being for Manchester City, the team who were not doing their stuff. But Burnley were a lovely side, and I remember Jimmy McIlroy dribbling in a figure of eight by the corner flag during the last twenty minutes as the score suited Burnley."

Burnley took an early lead in the game with a bizarre goal that deflected in off City's legendary German goalkeeper Bert Trautmann. The Manchester side equalised in front of 66,000 crowd to give Cullis hope, but Burnley were ahead again on the half-hour and despite a few late scares hung on for the title. "Naturally, I am disappointed. But I don't wish to make any further comment." said Cullis after the game.

The mood of some players was more relaxed. Bill Slater recalled: "We were so close to a marvellous achievement, yet I don't recall there being any talk of the possibility of winning The Double among the players. I listened to the Burnley game on the radio I think, and of course we were very disappointed when it wasn't the right result for us."

Five days later Wolves had the chance to brush away their disappointment at Wembley. Many stories are told about that 1960 Cup Final. There was Blackburn striker Derek Dougan making a transfer request public on the morning of the match. There was Rovers defender Dave Whelan, later to become a multi-millionaire owner of the JJB sports shop chain, taken off injured, leaving his side down to ten men. There was the worried reaction of the football authorities to fans throwing rubbish at the players as they left the field. There was the tale of a classic Stan Cullis comment to his South African winger Des Horne, as told by Ken Jones of the

Daily Mirror. "At that time Wembley had a huge advert for the *Radio Times* on the scoreboards at each end," said Jones. "Stan's instruction to Horne, who wasn't the brightest of players, was that when Wolves got the ball he was to start running in the direction of the 'R' in *Radio Times* and a team-mate would send a forward pass for him to chase.

Cullis took a risk on using the inexperienced Barry Stobart at inside right for the match, and it paid off as Stobart had a fine game. Yet the reaction of the Wolves manager to plaudits afterwards was typical of the Cullis ethos. He said: "Whenever we make a gamble and it comes off I always say thank goodness. When they call me a genius, they little realise how near it is to calling me a fool. They'd have hung, drawn and quartered me if it hadn't come off."

The match, especially once Whelan was injured, proved a simple victory for Wolves as their manager, wearing sunglasses on a bright afternoon, munched his way through a bag of sweets on the bench to try to calm his nerves. They took the lead thanks to an own goal by Mick McGrath, and then two strikes from Norman Deeley gave them a 3-0 victory and some compensation for missing out on the League title.

In those days reporters were allowed into the Wembley dressing-rooms after Cup Finals to get a quick reaction to events. Novelist and football writer Brian Glanville captured the scene.

> "Cullis turns to someone and says: 'Have you got my Vaseline to keep my hair down? Where's my chapeau?' He retrieves it from a peg, and blows dust off it. 'Been on the floor a few times.' At least you've got the Cup someone asks. 'It's a flopping nuisance, I can tell you. You have to send it to this fete and that fete.'"

The detailed observations on the mood and preoccupations of Cullis are fascinating. Everything must be just so, while a worldly cynicism fills his conversation. Elation is conspicuous by its absence. This mood was deliberate, as he later explained. "I remember the press photographers wanted me to do a lap of honour afterwards but I refused," he said. "I didn't want to take any limelight away from the players. And when the cameramen asked for a picture of me drinking champagne in the dressing-room I had to say no again. I didn't drink champagne. I offered to pose drinking a cup of tea but they weren't very impressed. They said their sports editors would have gone mad at seeing a Cup-winning manager drinking tea!"

Bill Slater remembered the traditional post-match banquet he attended after climbing the 39 Wembley steps to the Royal Box to collect the FA Cup trophy. He said: "We went to the celebration dinner in London. Stan stood up to make a speech, said all the things you might expect about the great honour of winning, and then finished with a typical comment. He reminded us exactly when pre-season training was due to start, and ordered us to ensure we kept in good condition through the summer break. Even then he wouldn't let up."

There was a softer, sentimental side to the character of Stan Cullis, however. At that same dinner he and Bill Holden of the *Daily Mirror*, a Black Country man from Bloxwich, talked about the fact that the Man from the Mirror had become a father three days earlier, when his son was born. Cullis agreed a high-spirited deal that the baby boy would be signed up by him there and then for the Wolves. Thus the author's passion for football was ensured.

The next season Wolves would finish third in the League table, despite scoring 103 goals. Cullis's frustration must have been immense as that year Tottenham Hotspur finally became the first club to secure the elusive Double. It gave them a place in soccer legend that Cullis always felt should have been the preserve of Wolverhampton Wanderers.

Little did anyone imagine it at the time, but victory in the 1960 Cup Final was the last triumph of Stan Cullis as a football manager. His two FA Cup wins marked the beginning and end of the glory years of the Wolves. The club sandwich was filled with three League titles and a host of memorable European nights.

After many big games Cullis would be interviewed on Sports Report by its then presenter Eamonn Andrews. Stan's son Andrew remembers listening to the exchanges time and again on the radio at the family home in Wolverhampton. "We knew what his first words would be every time," recalled Andrew. "He'd say: 'Well, Eamonn, I haven't got a crystal ball'. We'd tease him all the time about that. He always said it."

A crystal ball gazer in May 1960 would certainly not have anticipated the almost instant decline of Stan Cullis's football team.

Chapter Nine

Betrayal

"...don't let the actions of some very small people get you down..." Stanley Matthews

STAN Cullis demanded total control of playing affairs and team matters at the Wolves. While they enjoyed never-ending years of success through the 1950s, and while Cullis had a marvellous working relationship with long-serving Molineux chairman Joe Baker, he was given the absolute authority he knew to be imperative for a football manager. When the team's fortunes began to slide in the first few seasons of the 1960s, his authoritarian style began to look less attractive to ambitious new directors. One such was John Ireland, a secondhand car dealer in Wolverhampton and, ironically, the man who had sent Cullis a wartime letter wondering whether he had considered becoming manager of Wolves at that time.

Ireland's thoughts about the Cullis style no doubt developed gradually, but one incident in particular may be seen as the beginning of the end for The Iron Manager. It was vividly described by England half-back Eddie Clamp in a newspaper column years later looking back on his time at Molineux.

"We had lost 5-1 at Luton and Cullis came out of the ground black and scowling," wrote Clamp. "He practically marched us out of the dressing-room into the team coach. 'Peter Broadbent missing' said trainer Joe Gardiner as the coach door slammed. 'Go without him' snapped Cullis. The coach was halfway to Luton station when the driver piped up, 'Mr Ireland is missing'. 'Go without him too' ordered Cullis. But when we reached the station Broadbent and director Ireland were waiting on the platform, They had nipped ahead of us in a taxi after discovering Cullis had abandoned them at the ground. John Ireland was the newest Wolves director but he wasn't standing for any nonsense from a manager. All of the players watched this almost unknown director walk up to Cullis and tackle him immediately. 'Just remember in future' said Ireland, 'that you're not dealing with your schoolboy players when you deal with me, Mr Cullis'. I felt like cheering. It was the first time any of us had seen Stan put in his place. And I couldn't help remembering the incident when Stan was sensationally sacked."

Cullis himself recalled two other similar occasions. When he missed a match against Manchester City at Maine Road because he was away scouting for a new player, Ireland had taken advantage of his absence to go into the dressing-room at half-time to berate the players, an action he must have known would rile the Iron Manager because directors had been expressly banned from doing that at Wolves since before the war and the days of Major Buckley. Cullis was enraged and insisted that it would never happen again.

In the summer of 1963, though, he lost the next direct power battle with Ireland, who had created a strong alliance with the then chairman James Marshall. Ireland wanted to take his wife on a close-season summer tour to the USA and Canada, and this time he was successful. Looking back Cullis felt this was significant, as had been the departure of his long-term ally, the previous chairman, Joe Baker.

"Mr Baker, a sick man, resigned in August 1962, and he died five months later," said Cullis. "It was a sad loss to Wolves and I now felt unhappy for the first time during my long stay at Molineux. It was the beginning of the end for Stan Cullis."

Other factors, however, were involved apart from this clash of personality and character with Ireland. The abolition of the maximum wage in 1961 undoubtedly made it more difficult for a manager like Cullis to operate successfully. When players had flexed their muscles against the football establishment and emerged victorious after a High Court case in the most significant financial battle in the history of the English game, it was obvious that their deference to authority would be affected. The bark of Cullis could not be accompanied by as much bite as in the past. The players were beginning to realise the power they could wield.

He recognised that himself in an observation about the changing attitudes, saying: "It was always my policy to give players the right to express themselves. I listened carefully to every word, especially when they disagreed with my ideas. These discussions often went on for many hours with men like Billy Wright, Bill Slater and the players of the 1950s – and the benefit was reaped on the field. But towards the end of my thirty years at Molineux I found the tactical talks were getting shorter and shorter. It became difficult to get players to express themselves, and frankly I was baffled. Then two players who came to see me on the subject told me somewhat sheepishly that certain members of the team had made it clear they didn't want lengthy tactical talks which delayed their departure from the ground."

Cullis also found it harder this time to ensure a smooth transition of newcomers as key players like Slater retired from the game. A sentence Cullis wrote in *All For The Wolves* in 1960 resonates deeply. "Inevitably, the most successful of clubs will run into bad times," said Cullis. "In transitional periods, when key players are dropping out through age and youngsters are taking over, a club which has held a high position for several years can easily drop into the lower half of the table. It is strange that a manager should lose his job simply because some of his stars have grown old – but it happens."

The words were eerily prophetic. In the 1961-62 season Wolves finished in eighteenth place, only four points above the two relegation places. The next year appeared to have solved the problems as they ended fifth, scoring 93 goals. But the 1963-64 season saw another slump to sixteenth place. Yet Stan Cullis still did not see himself as a potential victim of the process he described above. He remained convinced that the success and glory he had brought to Molineux would be restored using his sound, tried and trusted principles of management.

Before the start of the 1964-65 season Cullis spoke at the club's annual meeting. He had been linked in the Press with the managerial vacancy at Sheffield Wednesday, but told the audience: "I will never leave Wolves unless I am sacked." They were not the words of man who thought he would be out of a job within six weeks, although John Ireland surely noted the sentiment.

The season began badly, with a succession of defeats that left Wolves bottom of the table with no points. Cullis was unwell, too, and he recalled the time in a *News of the World* article written after his dismissal at Molineux. "It all began on Friday, 28 August when I fainted at my desk," wrote Cullis. "I went home after the club doctor attended to me and, believe it or not, very soon it was around Wolverhampton that Stan Cullis had died of a heart attack."

His doctor ordered him to take a few weeks rest by the seaside at Eastbourne, just as he had been ordered to rest on medical advice in the summer of 1956. Son Andrew believes it may have been a mild stroke; the symptoms were similar to those his father suffered in later years. The pressure of football management is always relentless, but no-one suffered more from it than Stan Cullis. He gave his heart and soul to the job, and when results were poor the pressure he felt can only have intensified.

Cullis returned from his holiday on Monday, 14 September 1964. While he had been away the seeds of discontent sown over the past few years had been harvested in his absence. Once, when the players had made a general transfer request and leaked it to the Press, Cullis faced them down by force of character, daring them to defy him personally. They could not do it. Now, however, as an element among the playing staff made noises again, a powerful leader of rebellion had emerged in the shape of John Ireland, who had become chairman of the club.

That Monday night, with Stan Cullis directing operations on the bench, Wolves beat West Ham 4-3 in a thrilling match. By kick-off time he already knew that it would be his final game in charge of the club he had joined more than thirty years earlier. In early afternoon the shock was still to come because he gave an interview to Ken Jones of the *Daily Mirror*, who had come up to talk to the returning manager. "Stan was talking about his plans, about how he would try to get the team up the table as quickly as possible," recalled Jones. "He cannot have known then. A couple of days later, when he was still too upset to talk about the sacking, I rang him at home. He wouldn't come to the phone, but told his wife Winifred to let me know that when he had spoken he had no idea what was coming."

But Cullis later explained the sequence of events in an article for the *News of the World*, revealing: "I was sitting at my desk that Monday when Mr John Ireland came into my office and without even inquiring about my health greeted me with this comment, 'I must tell you the Board no longer have any confidence in you'.

"He then suggested I should resign for health reasons. I was dumbfounded, but I refused to be involved in anything that wasn't accurate, and said: 'If you want to sack me you must tell the truth'. It seemed to me that Mr Ireland, while wanting to chop off my head, preferred a bloodless execution to avoid embarrassment. All nice, clean, tidy stuff with handshakes all round. But I wasn't having any part of it. For as much it hurt my pride to be kicked out and labelled a failure after a lifetime with one club, I wouldn't be party to a subterfuge. Specialists had already given me a clean bill of health. So it was the sack or nothing. Mr Ireland's final comment on leaving my office was, 'I don't know what my wife will say when I tell her I've sacked you'. I wondered whether he was interested in what my wife would feel when I broke the bad news to her."

One amazing aspect is that on the Tuesday lunchtime, before the news had broken, Cullis kept a long-held promise to make a speech to the Wolverhampton Rotary Club. It was typical of his principled character. Ireland, who was a member of the Rotary Club, did not attend.

Jimmy Hill, then manager of Coventry, had become a close colleague of Cullis, and said: "Stan came through it all with great dignity. He sat through the West Ham game knowing it would be his last in charge of a Wolverhampton team, surely the dearest thing in life to him next to his own family. The following morning, knowing the news was going to break in the afternoon, he still kept his silence and went to the Rotary Club."

The sacking shocked football more deeply than any dismissal of a manager had done before, and few since. It shared the front pages of many national newspapers with the announcement by Prime Minister Sir Alec Douglas Home of the General Election, and it was barely believable to thousands of Wolves fans, both in the actual sacking of a man who had brought so much glory to the club, and in the manner of the deed when Cullis had just returned from sick leave.

Ireland's initial action was to make a brief statement to the Press. It read: "Wolverhampton Wanderers' board of directors has informed the manager, Mr Stan Cullis, that it wishes to be released from all contract arrangements with him, and that he has consented to do so."

If the Wolves chairman thought that was enough to satisfy anyone he was hugely mistaken. The sacking of Cullis caused an uproar in Wolverhampton, where hundreds of ordinary fans wrote letters to Cullis himself and to the *Express and Star* newspaper bitterly denouncing the move. It also caused immense shock through the wider world of English football. Amid a stream of letters received by Cullis, these give a flavour of the mood.

From: Johnson, Prisoner 722 Wormwood Scrubs: "Dear Mr Cullis. I am sure you will get many letters similar to this, but not many with the above line of address! I have not always agreed with your published opinions as manager but I remember you as a player since your first appearance at Stamford Bridge before the war and held you in high regard from that time. Your sacking should not have happened."

From: Dennis Wilshaw: "No-one could have done more for Wolves. You have helped me and many more like me to a happy career in the game, and your dedication, honesty and high character have made a profound mark upon my life. I am proud that I have worked with you for, I like to think, your standards have become my standards. Your achievements will never be surpassed and I know your courage will see you safely through this black cloud which has suddenly descended."

From Stanley Matthews: "Knowing each other as we do, you will not want or expect me to write platitudes. So all I will say is not to lose faith in something which you believe, and not to let the actions of some very small people get you down."

From: Matt Busby: "I am still trying to recover from the shock of yesterday's announcement. It has knocked me sick of human nature. How people could do such a thing after you giving them your life's blood? What more success can they get than what you've given them? What loyalty have they shown you after the loyalty you have given them in every way? Oh, I could go on and on. Anyway, Stan, please accept my sincere sympathies, and whatever you decide to do in the future may it abound with happiness and success in the wish of Your Friend, Matt."

The emotion of Busby's message needs no amplification. Cullis's closest friend in football, a man of equal stature in the game, could not believe it. His team endured the odd poor season, but would Manchester United ever have sacked him? John Giles, a player at United in the early 1960s, believes it was possible, saying: "We had a slump for a few seasons in the early sixties just as Wolves did. My recollection is that there was some pressure on Matt, but it disappeared when we won the FA Cup in 1963 and of course he built a new team that won the European Cup a few years later. What would Wolves have done if Stan Cullis had been given more time? Who knows? But I do remember being very shocked when he was sacked. I thought Stan was a god as a football man, a giant of the game. At the time I couldn't believe that Wolves would sack a man like him. Later that season I was with Leeds, having moved clubs that summer, and we won at Molineux. It wasn't the same place without Stan Cullis."

The letter from Matthews is poignant too. They had been contemporaries as players before the war, both chosen at a young age for England. What a contrast now. Cullis had been sacked after sixteen years as a manager – Matthews was still playing First Division football for Stoke City.

There were so many other letters in similar vein, too, from men like former England manager Walter Winterbottom and 'push and run' Spurs manager Arthur Rowe. The reaction was so fierce that John Ireland was forced to issue a public justification of his action. It only served to inflame the situation further. Three days later Ireland issued a second statement which said the directors were unanimous and spoke of "serious problems which existed within the club. Matters were recently brought to a head by complaints and transfer requests from a number of established players, which forced the board to the belief that this position was brought about by the treatment of the players by the manager, and who, they felt, no longer had the confidence and respect of the players. The directors felt this situation called for immediate and drastic action."

It is a fact that some players had made transfer requests, but that was nothing new. It is common enough in football clubs, particularly those where confidence and morale has been affected by poor results. If the players were implicated in the decision, they certainly weren't consulted. Half-back Ron Flowers, one Wolves star who had asked for a transfer, said: "The players were told nothing. We read it in the papers."

Cullis's initial desire was to hold his tongue. He confined himself that Tuesday to a brief explanation of his emotions. He told the *Daily Mirror*: "Football, like many other professions, is a hard world. One has to be tough. Tough? Maybe resilient is a better word. Thirty years is a long time. But this is life and one has to accept it. I would rather not comment on how or when I was given the news. I don't think it would be fair. Now it's all over. I was absent with a virus infection, but am completely fit and was given a clean bill of health. It was a wonderful thing when a man has served an organisation for thirty years, is taken ill, and comes back to this. And no word of thanks."

No word of thanks for three League titles, two FA Cups, and countless nights of muddy magic against the giants of Europe. To sack Cullis was bad enough. To do so with such brutal disrespect was a crime that Cullis has never forgiven.

Ireland's statement on the Friday prompted a further response from the Iron Manager, rebutting some of the central allegations of the Wolves chairman. It read:

> "I wish to say I feel sorry that the players have been used to justify the actions of the directors. The statement that it was a unanimous decision was hardly consistent with two directors informing me they had strenuously fought the suggestion to sack me at special meeting which lasted five hours. At no time was I given an opportunity to discuss the matter at a board meeting with the directors. I requested this to Mr Ireland, but he refused. Two weeks before my dismissal I was told by directors they were getting down to drafting a new contract despite my present contract not being due for renewal. Mr Ireland suggested I should resign, either for health reasons or over differences of opinions with the board. I told him that if my reputation would not stand up to my being sacked I was certainly not going to tell a lie. If I'd agreed to what had been suggested I would have been telling an outright lie – and I wouldn't do that for anyone."

Here is another reason why Stan Cullis was so bitter about the sacking. John Ireland obviously had no idea of the nature of his manager by asking him to lie for convenience sake. Cullis was utterly appalled by the request. The rift was total, and Ireland continued to pile on the indignity. Only half a dozen lines in the next Wolves match programme acknowledged the end of Stan Cullis's managerial career at Molineux.

A few days later he received a letter from the club. It read: "Dear Stan, I have been instructed by the Chairman to request you to let me have your keys of the Club. Yours Sincerely, The Secretary." On the letter head of the official Wolverhampton Wanderers notepaper it was still inscribed with Stanley Cullis - Manager. A line of faint XXXs had been typed over the name - but had signally failed to obscure Stanley Cullis as intended. That was symbolically appropriate.

Wolves then even asked Cullis to pay them back the sum of £4 to cover the advance rental on his phone from October to December 1964. The level of pettiness is almost unbelievable.

Ireland's decision did not work out as he intended. Wolves were bottom of the table and remained in the relegation zone throughout that 1964-65 season and were demoted to Division Two the next spring. The new manager, Andy Beattie, a man dubbed 'The Flying Doctor' because he was often employed in this kind of circumstance, had an impossible task. Crowds slumped at Molineux and not just because the team were playing badly. Many hundreds of fans actually refused to watch because of the way Cullis had been treated. It is a cliche of football to hear fans say they will tear up their season tickets in disgust. In this case it was exactly what happened. It seemed symbolic, too, that Cullis's mentor, Major Frank Buckley, died during that bleak winter for Wolves.

The sacking of such a mighty figure in football brought an inevitable rash of analysis in the Press. In the *Daily Mirror*, Ken Jones, who had worked closely with Cullis in ghosting a number of articles in newspapers, wrote: "Cullis's problems were the problems of soccer's changing times. His success was built on long-ball attacks and fighting forwards who could turn the power passes into goals. When the flow of players stopped from the Wolves system of scouts, Cullis was forced to spend. He did not always spend well. It wasn't easy to buy men who could fit into the Wolves pattern. And the pattern didn't fit with the more mature method demanded by the modern game."

Others noted the process whereby players, following the lifting of the maximum wage, were becoming unhappy with the authoritarian style of management epitomised by Cullis. "Fat wage packets make for thin skins," wrote Hugh McIlvanney in *The Observer* as he reflected on the departure of the Iron Manager.

David Miller, then writing for the *Sunday Telegraph*, observed: "There had been talk for eighteen months that Cullis would have to watch his step if Jack Ireland become chairman. Cullis knew about this talk. But no-one could have foreseen that the sacking would have been done with such inhumanity and lack of conviction, and with no warning to Cullis. Jack Ireland did not even remove his pipe when interviewed on TV about a matter that touched the lives of thousands of people." Miller also shared the feeling that the authoritarian Cullis style was rapidly becoming impossible, adding: "Youngsters of today won't accept the same iron discipline that players in the 1940s and 50s would."

In Wolverhampton the *Express and Star* newspaper was regarded as gospel, and it remains a giant among local provincial evening newspapers around England. It said: "Cullis told us what he regarded as one of the reasons for the current slump. He put it down to the failure to be able to compete for young players. It is well known in football that clubs were going "under the counter" for the best youngsters and this was something Wolves would never do. They abided by the rules and Cullis felt they were now paying the penalty."

Cullis himself was keen to make that point too. Three weeks after his sacking, in a series of articles for the *News of the World*, he said this: "Let's get the record straight. It was no lack of foresight on my part that put Wolves in their present position. Six years ago in 1958 when we were League champions I told my directors that the way things were going in the game we would be in a sticky spell for years to come because so many clubs were indulging in illegal payments. So many of them were bribing the top schoolboy talent, always the main source of supply at Molineux, with fantastic financial offers to parents. Wolves directors decided that no matter what other clubs did we would not be a party to any such under-the-counter methods. I agreed, but said I hoped they would remember my warning when things started going wrong."

Six days can be a long time in football. To expect football club directors to remember a point made six years earlier was entirely futile. The Iron Manager knew that, of course, but his integrity was total, and he wanted the point made public.

Most of his friends in the game rallied instantly. On the first Saturday in thirty years when Cullis did not have a job in football, he was invited to watch Second Division Coventry City play at home to Northampton by the Sky Blues manager Jimmy Hill, who, ironically, had been a leading campaigner as head of the Players' Union for the abolition of the maximum wage. Hill waxed indignant in the Coventry programme, and Cullis did some scouting work for Hill in the following few months.

Hill was mentioned as a possible successor to Cullis at Molineux before Beattie accepted the job, but in a newspaper article, said: "It certainly won't be me. I don't think any football club can gain from losing Stan Cullis. His store of soccer knowledge is unsurpassed and, what's more, he is a straight-forward man, loyal to the point of fanaticism, worthy to an extent which must at times have amazed some of those with whom he did business. I thought of all that when he sat beside me at Coventry the first Saturday after he was sacked, and he told me, 'you know Jim, I am not ashamed of anything I have done and I see no reason why I should not hold my head up and face the world'."

Cullis vented his true feelings in the *News of the World* the following week, saying: "I'm no longer angry, but I'm still disgusted at my treatment by Wolverhampton Wanderers – a club I served as player, captain and manager for more than thirty years. To be sacked on my first day back after sick leave is something that I would never have done to the most junior member of my staff." A deep bitterness towards Ireland has never left Stan Cullis.

Former Wolves players of stature also paid tribute to their manager. Bill Slater said: "The sacking from Wolves upset him a great deal, and it upset many of his old players too. I didn't want to go to the club for a while after that happened, and I wasn't alone in my view. It was no way to treat a man who had given everything to Wolves. There had to have been a better way to deal with the situation."

Billy Wright put his thoughts down in a newspaper column,

too, saying: "Stan was the complete perfectionist. Nothing but the best was enough. He was one of the greatest managers of all time, and one of the greatest centre-halves to stride across a football pitch. My ears still ring with some of the verbal blastings he handed out during dressing-room briefings that set even the toughest of players shaking at the knees. He was tough and ruthless. He was 100 per cent dedicated to the Wolves and expected the same approach from his players. His greatest quality was dedication. Perhaps his greatest weakness was that too. Dedication – too much dedication."

No-one at Molineux knew Cullis better than his former skipper. He had worried about his manager's health in the mid-1950s and now felt sure that Cullis had driven himself into the ground with his burning obsession to succeed.

What dismayed Stan Cullis about the sacking was the reaction of a few of his closest colleagues at Wolves. Daughter Susan said: "My father was deeply upset by the response of some people at the club who dropped him because it wasn't politic at Molineux to keep in touch the former manager. He took it very badly and I am sure it contributed to the rift with the club that remained for years."

We have already seen how Cullis was rarely at home as football consumed his life. Now he had time on his hands, and was thankful for the strong support of his wife Winifred and his son and daughter. Winifred had never seen so much of him – and agreed to give the only interview of her life to a newspaper, to the local *Express and Star*. The clipping was kept in the family collection for posterity. Stan's loyal wife told the interviewer that she had agreed to speak because of "the desk which we can't close because the letters are piled so high." The cutting has a photograph of the mountain of letters to prove how extraordinary the response had been to the sacking.

"It's only just this last week or so that I've realised what my husband's done for football," said Winifred Cullis. "That's absolutely true. Look at all the letters, some from people we've never heard of. There's even one from a man at Wormwood Scrubs. With all his troubles he's found time to write to Stan. Isn't that wonderful. Those letters have been one of the most warming things to me. In the home I have to make the decisions. So often, because of his work, he's not been here. I've kept the domestic problems from him. That's been my responsibility. The wife of someone who has a football career obviously has to be prepared to be alone a lot."

It was recognition of her role in the Stan Cullis story. Like any good journalist the lady from the *Express and Star* tried to discover a few human interest angles. What was Stan's favourite dish? "He loved apple pie," said Winifred proudly.

Daughter Susan remains proud of her mother's support for the Iron Manager. "She tried very hard to make sure that my father had a life away from his obsession with football. They had a social scene with friends, playing tennis and golf, and they loved going dancing. My father also loved listening to opera and bought many records. His favourite was *Madame Butterfly*, and he even had a version in Russian acquired on one of his trips with the Wolves.

"I also remember how it was important for the family to be seen at the Wolves games. We would go to every match, even when the reserves played. There was a tremendous feeling of comradeship and fellow feeling in the town that came from the football club's success. You sensed it strongly when you walked into Molineux. It was something quite special, and I was proud that my father had done so much to create that."

After the initial shock had subsided, there came the question of what Stan Cullis would do next. In the modern world of the media, such speculation is instant. The story in the next day's paper would be which club a sacked manager might go to next rather than just the mere news of his sacking. In Cullis's day such looking to the future took a week or two longer to develop. In his case the interest was impressive. Although he had been the manager of Wolves for sixteen years, he was still only 47 years old. He had a worldwide reputation as one of the great football men and that was reflected in job offers.

The first club to express an interest was Sunderland, who had a ready-made vacancy for a big-name boss. Don Revie, then manager of Leeds, had already applied for it, but had been refused permission to speak to the Roker Park chairman. What a farsighted move that was at Elland Road. If any club inherited the mantle of Wolves in the next ten years it was Leeds United under Revie's intelligent and tough leadership.

Another candidate might have been Jimmy Adamson, the manager of Burnley, the club that had so narrowly prevented Wolves from winning the Double a few seasons earlier. Their voluble chairman Bob Lord, dubbed the Butcher of Burnley, reacted just as Leeds had and denied Adamson permission to speak to Sunderland, whose reaction was declare an interest in Cullis.

That admission brought an extraordinary response from Lord, who wrote privately to Stan Cullis. The letter is worth recording exactly as sent:

> "What I would like to know is: where is there a manager who has done for one club what you have done for Wolves? Further, is there left in the game a MAN who is self-respecting who would take over the position you have vacated at Wolverhampton? I suspect there are plenty of fools who would, and so we go on. Most of the men on club's boards make me heartily sick when I listen to them, likewise most of them I am certain are made of pulp, no guts and precious little football know-how. Stan, my heart bled for you when I heard the news, likewise did it bleed for the game, which is being crucified.
>
> "Finally, one word of warning from a straight bloke to another straight bloke, have no truck with the Sunderland set-up."

There is a little more of this letter, but further allegations by Lord against the Roker regime are too scurrilous to print. Whether the warning was needed or not, Stan Cullis rejected the chance to become manager at Sunderland.

The next bout of newspaper speculation reflected the prestige of Cullis in Europe, where despite their 9-2 aggregate failure against Barcelona in the 1959-60 European Cup quarter-final, the name of Wolverhampton Wanderers continued to be held in high esteem. The story in the *Daily Express* proclaimed that he had been made a £10,000 a year offer to become the manager of Italian club Juventus, based in Turin.

Cullis was quoted in the article, written by his old tormentor Desmond Hackett, saying: "I am considering this offer very seriously. I have been invited to go to Turin to look at Juventus for a month, or for as long as I wish, because there is no urgency about taking over this position. I speak soldier's Italian from the War, and I think I could get by with that."

The owner of Juventus, Giovanni Agnelli, whose family also ran the Fiat motor firm in the city, was also quoted in the clipping that Cullis kept in his collection. Agnelli said: "We would prefer to adopt his system of discovering and maturing our own players. The European and South American way of football is killing the game. It has become a set pattern with such emphasis on defence that the whole thing is becoming a bore. I feel sure Mr Cullis is capable of recreating the old excitements. The hard expert way of English football is going to be the only way to bring back the audiences."

This was less than two years before England would win the 1966 World Cup with that hard and expert passion instilled by Sir Alf Ramsey, who had succeeded Winterbottom as England manager. At one time Cullis had also been mentioned as a possible candidate. How strong the interest from Juventus was, we cannot know. Italian clubs liked to give themselves a few options when a change of coach was coming. Many Englishmen had prospered abroad, like George Raynor, who took Sweden to the 1958 World Cup Final. Whether Cullis could have translated his style to the highly political arena of Italian football is a question we can't answer.

What he did was decide to take a break from management following his dismissal at Wolves. It had shocked him to the core; his whole adult life, and much of the football talk in his boyhood, perhaps, had been The Wolves. A swift move elsewhere would not be appropriate, and there was also his health to consider. While Cullis publicly proclaimed his renewed strength, there must have been private concerns within the family.

Cullis still needed to work, however. Managers then were not paid extravagant sums, although his existence was more than comfortable, and he could afford to send his son and daughter to Public School. He agreed to contribute a series of articles to the *News Of The World* about his thoughts on football, and took on the job he had considered as a boy back in Ellesmere Port – journalism. He became a football reporter for the *News Of The World*, covering Saturday afternoon matches in the League he had once dominated as a manager.

That led to a chance conversation reported by Arthur Hopcraft in his fine book *The Football Man*. Cullis said: "I was walking away from the office and a man stopped me. He was a Londoner. He said: 'You're Stan Cullis, aren't you?' He said: 'Me and my wife are Arsenal supporters. Do you know what? When Arsenal are playing away we can't wait to find out how they've got on. But the next thing we look for is to see how Wolves got on. If they've lost we go out and have a drink. What they did to you was shocking.'"

In the same book the Iron Manager had distance of time to look a little more reflectively on his downfall at Molineux. "Looking back," he said: "I'd only created a yardstick that people could criticise me against. I knew it was only a question of time."

That is the conventional modern view of football management – that the only certainty is the sack. Perhaps one way of looking at Stan Cullis's thirty years at Wolves as player and manager is to reflect on how few football men give such long service to one club. In the *News Of The World* annual there is a section on this issue. Top of their list is Bob Paisley, who joined Liverpool as a player in 1939 and remained at the club until his death in 1996 in a variety of roles including manager. Ernie Gregory gets a mention with West Ham, where he began as a young player in 1935 and retired as a coach in 1987. Others who are listed include Roy Sproson, 21 years at Port Vale, and Ted Sagar, 23 years as a goalkeeper at Everton. Stan Cullis is not mentioned despite his thirty years. It is another small indication of shameful neglect.

With the benefit of hindsight it hardly takes great wisdom to deduce that the sacking of Cullis was both foolish and wrong as well as cruelly engineered. Its ostensible immediate purpose, to keep Wolves in the First Division, failed miserably. It alienated a significant number of fans, and despite a brief flicker of success in the mid-1970s when the club won the League Cup and reached the Final of the UEFA Cup, Wolverhampton Wanderers have ceased to be one of England's leading clubs. At one stage they had plummeted to the old Fourth Division.

The dismissal of Cullis did much more than just put a football manager out of work. It destroyed the values on which Wolves had been based from Major Frank Buckley in the 1930s through to the heydays of the 1950s. Stan Cullis gave his all for the Wolves, yet in 1967, when he had become manager of neighbouring Birmingham City, he was asked about his feelings for the club. The bitterness remained in his soul, and he said: "Put it this way. Nothing would give me greater pleasure than to take my team there in the First Division and beat them."

Chapter Ten

A Job Too Far

"...He wouldn't suffer fools gladly. He was one for correctness in all things..." Walter Winterbottom

THE Passionate Puritan had the shock of his life one day when he took his son Andrew to a match at West Bromwich Albion. Andrew Cullis, who had been told as a young boy by his father that he would never be good enough to make the grade as a professional footballer, had been studying engineering at university. However, he had decided he wanted to become a vicar – of which he informed his father as they were watching this particular game at The Hawthorns.

"His reaction was to be very surprised," said Andrew. "He looked perplexed and said to me, 'That's a funny old job being a vicar, isn't it?'. 'Not as funny as being a football manager,' I said back to him. 'At least you don't get the sack!' 'Point taken,' he said. I remember as well that he was very put out a few days afterwards when he told some friends that I was going into the church. One of them was surprised and said to Stan, 'Not a bit like you then'. My father was upset. He was very like me, but that wasn't his public image. That shook him a bit."

Stan Cullis's obsession with creating a great football team for Wolverhampton had blinded him to much in life, as it does so many managers of leading soccer clubs. The attitude may be summed up by Bill Shankly's immortal line about 'football not being a matter of life and death – it's more important than that'.

Of course, Cullis had enjoyed a few hobbies away football. He played golf, as did his wife Winifred; he was a 13-handicapper. He also played cricket quite regularly for the Wolves team in charity matches and for the South Staffs club; he was said to be a dour batsman at the crease but a brilliant fielder. He loved opera and dancing and was a voracious reader of books, particularly about military history, so much so that in November 1963, while still manager of the Wolves and one of the most well-known faces in England, Cullis wrote what seems an extraordinary autograph hunter's letter to his own great hero.

To Viscount Field Marshall Montgomery of Alamein K.G.

Dear Sir,

You will not remember me, but I had the honour of presenting the England and Army teams to you during the War, and I represented the Eighth Army soccer team when I was serving in Italy.

I have read your book three times and despite anything your critics say, I am sure the men who served under you will never forget the drive and inspiration you gave them during the War.

As one of your many admirers, I hope you will not mind me forwarding the book for your personal signature.

Yours faithfully,
Stanley Cullis,
Manager.

The great wartime general returned his autobiography by return of post, suitably inscribed, and added a note to the bottom of Cullis's own letter, saying: "Certainly. I have signed the book. I have never seen The Wolves play. I wish your team all success in the present season. Montgomery of Alamein."

That was a rare diversion for Stan Cullis. The job of managing Wolves had consumed his existence, and now to have so much spare time was demanding on his desire to achieve and succeed in a very different way. Saturday afternoons were usefully spent working as a football writer for the *News Of The World*. As a young man he had toyed with the idea of journalism, and before the War he had sat in the press box sometimes when he was rested from a match.

Many sportswriters have told me their opinion that Cullis had little time for their breed. Yet his son Andrew and daughter Susan both told me how fond he was of journalists. "He really liked them," said Susan. "I remember how he would spend most of Sunday afternoon on the phone talking to football reporters, much to the dismay of my mother."

Of course there is always a certain tension in the relationship between manager and the reporter who has to criticise when that is necessary. Cullis could also be a forbidding presence in the wrong mood, more than able to chastise a sportswriter who had written an article that he felt was untrue. But he respected the trade, saying: "I would frequently get telephone calls at home in the evenings or on Sundays from writers. It was not unknown for the bedside phone to ring after midnight. But I did not begrudge the time spent talking to the press." Cullis took great care over the words he used to describe football games, understanding very clearly the power they had to sway the mood of football fans.

Eventually, of course, the lure of football management had to take hold again. He had been out of the game for less than a year when Clifford Coombs, the chairman of Birmingham City began to make a serious approach to secure the Iron Manager. The pair were friends and St Andrew's was close enough to Wolverhampton that Cullis would not necessarily have to move house or area to take up the position.

Birmingham were a mid-table second division side then, as they have been for much of their history, but ambitious to reach the top flight. Cullis looked an ideal appointment. Son Andrew remembers the time vividly, saying: "My father had initially been offered the Birmingham job in the summer, and one day he said we should go along and have a look at what they are like. It was early September. We got in the car and he disguised himself with a heavy overcoat, dark glasses and big hat – he looked like a KGB agent. We arrived at the ground and queued up to buy a ticket. and someone in the crowd shouted out, 'Hello Mr Cullis.' My dad looked quite surprised and this chap said: 'I recognised your son from playing at the tennis club.' He had gone to all this trouble but he stood out a mile and it was laughable really. We watched the game sitting in the stand near the goal. Jim Herriott was the goalie and he was so casual, and that annoyed my father who couldn't abide that in a footballer."

Stan Cullis took his time considering whether to join Birmingham, but eventually returned to the dug-out on Boxing Day 1965, around fifteen months after his sacking at Molineux. It seemed an odd time to start, but perhaps appropriate to his attitude that the job came first. "I don't find Christmas any different to other times of the year," he said in a newspaper interview that week. "Perhaps I am too wrapped up in the game."

It was a telling comment. Although, maybe, that lack of sentimentality about Christmas was also a relic of his childhood days too.

Many letters arrived at the family home and his new office at the St Andrew's ground to celebrate Cullis's return to the game. His collection has literally hundreds of messages of support from the fans of Wolverhampton Wanderers. They were just ordinary supporters who wanted him to know how they felt. There is also a poignant short letter from 'Syd, and all at No.16 St Andrew's Rd, Ellesmere Port, Wirral'. It reads: "Dear Stan, Congratulations and all the best luck in your new job. Regards Syd." It was from his brother.

Former Wolves players like Roy Swinbourne and Dennis Wilshaw also wrote to wish him good fortune in the new job, as did former Arsenal centre-half turned journalist Bernard Joy. The theme was similar; delight that he was back following the callous treatment at Molineux.

Another letter that Cullis kept, most probably from a sense of wry amusement, came from an official of the Rediffusion electricals company. He wrote to Mr Callis (sic) to say "how delighted" he was to see Stan back in football management. It came with a PS, which said: "By the way, if the PA system ever wants renewing at Birmingham, you might like to consider this company. We have already covered Wembley Stadium."

Cullis could hardly be said to have jumped into the job, but he still arrived at Birmingham as an outsider, a totally different scenario to his move into management at Molineux, where the transition had been gradual through a year running the reserves. It was also a very different time at which he took over. The atmosphere of the Swinging Sixties in general and the abolition of the maximum wage in particular had caused a revolution in the attitude of players. That made it far harder for a football manager, particularly one steeped in old-fashioned ways and imbued with conservative attitudes, to impose his values on the players. Cullis's holy trinity of team spirit, fitness and efficient tactics would not be so readily accepted this time.

His approach on arrival was less severe than many at the club had expected and perhaps feared; surely an intelligent realisation on his part that the football world was changing, even if not necessarily for the better in his own view. It was also a response to the sacking at Wolves, after which he had said: "I am the first to admit human frailties in my own make up. I realised after what happened at Molineux that I ought to adopt a calmer attitude when watching matches."

One man who knew him well was Walter Winterbottom, the former England international manager who had played against Cullis as an opposition centre-half for Manchester United before the war. He had written to Cullis when he was sacked at Wolves, and remembered the change of approach engendered by time out of the game, saying: "Stan had more understanding of situations as he got older. He had firm opinions, but I thought he was quite an understanding fellow. He used to talk vigorously and firmly about things, almost as if he had to have too strong a view. He wouldn't suffer fools gladly. He was one for correctness in all things."

A similar change was seen by David Exall, who was Birmingham's commercial manager at the time, and the man who worked most closely with Cullis through his spell at St Andrew's. He explained: "As a kid I had read and heard so much about Stan Cullis. My father took me to see the Wolves, and this character reigned supreme. He had an aura as far as the supporters were concerned. I found Stan a totally different character to the one I'd known only from legend at Wolves. Although he had the reputation of being a total autocrat, he was in fact a quiet and quite gentle person who got over his views and ideas by force of argument rather than by imposing his will. He could rationalise things very clearly and persuade you that his point of view was right. That was my biggest surprise.

"He never ever swore. Virtually every sentence contained flipping or flopping, but in three and a half years, on occasions bitterly provoked by more outrageous players like Bobby Thompson and Trevor Hockey, he never swore. While he was at Birmingham, Stan delegated most of the coaching to Joe Mallett, who was a former Nottingham Forest player and coach, and previously joint manager at St Andrew's. Stan was certainly never a tracksuit manager, but he was always very much in touch, spending much time with the coaches, even if he did not actively coach the players himself then."

Inevitably, there were conflicts with the younger and wilder generation, especially as the first couple of seasons brought steady improvement rather than the spectacular success which will always paper over divisions within a football club. David Exall recalled two such incidents with clarity.

"There are moments which stand out from Stan's time at Birmingham," said Exall. "An occasion I particularly remember was Johnny Schofield's testimonial match. Bobby Thompson had a blinding row with Stan. Thompson was an incredible character, and an aggressive type of player. Stan brought him off and accused him of not trying – and Thompson responded by saying it was only a testimonial game. There was certainly a scuffle – and, needless to say, Thompson never played for Birmingham again. Stan dealt with that in a quiet way, particularly all the bad publicity which surrounded it. He never seemed affected by it.

"Trevor Hockey was a one-off. He played for everybody, and was the first player ever to appear on all 92 grounds in the League. He was a tremendous character, a kind of football Beatle. He had the haircut and was a real handful; a lovely bloke, but a character who was totally at odds with Stan. He had Stan in apoplexy because he would turn up to training in the latest and flashiest sports cars. Once Hockey arrived and asked Stan to come and look outside in the car park at his latest car. 'It's a real club car' he said to Stan, having had the outside of the car totally covered with a royal blue carpet. Stan just stood there in amazement. He said to Trevor, 'You must be flipping mad'. He wasn't at home with that kind of showmanship. I always felt it was strange that he had players in the team who were so at odds with his sort of personality, but he coped with them well.

"Stan was a kind of father figure, the last of the era of football managers who always wore a suit. The players respected him, but didn't really get on with him. Trevor Hockey, for instance, called him 'Old Skinhead' – but never to his face."

The mood could not have been further from that Cullis had been able to engineer at Wolves. When he had started as a manager there most of the players were former team-mates who had admired him as their loyal captain. They also knew and respected his stature in the game generally from the War years. When he delivered consistent success at Molineux it brooked little argument.

One man who appreciated the difference in practical terms was Ron Atkinson, one of the Cullis Cubs of the 1950s. A decade later he was appalled by the attitudes he encountered when visiting St Andrew's as a member of the opposition team, saying: "I played against that team quite regularly and I remember one of the Birmingham players being very disrespectful to him. I had a go back at the player in question and told him that Stan Cullis was a legend and he had done nothing in the game to start having a pop at him. Maybe Stan didn't have the same motivation at Birmingham. And it takes time to bring young players through, which was his policy. They did reach a couple of cup semi-finals as well."

The first two seasons with Cullis in charge saw Birmingham finish tenth each time in the Second Division, with the 1966-67 campaign notable for two good cup runs. In the League Cup they went to the semi-finals of the League Cup, where the team self-destructed, losing home and away to Third Division Queen's Park Rangers, inspired by a real child of the Sixties, Rodney Marsh. The aggregate score was a humiliating 7-2 defeat. In the FA Cup the Blues reached the quarter-finals and fought out an epic 0-0 draw at home to Tottenham Hotspur before losing the replay 6-0 at White Hart Lane. Spurs went on to win at Wembley, just as QPR had done.

One of the directors of Birmingham at that time was Doug Ellis, another Ellesmere Port boy, and later to find fame as the chairman of Aston Villa, where he earned the nickname 'Deadly' for his habit of sacking football managers.

Cullis and Ellis became close friends, and Ellis remembered how he would drive the manager round the country in his Rolls-Royce. "I was Stan's chauffeur, so to speak," said Ellis. "I would go with him on scouting missions and we would talk about football constantly all the way. I learned so much about the game from Stan in those conversations. He knew the location of the best fish and chip shop in every football town in the country and after games he would insist we drove to it, even down small back streets in the Rolls-Royce. Every time it seemed there would be a queue of football club scouts waiting for their cod or haddock.

"I remember that one time we drove all the way to St Johnstone to watch a potential buy for Birmingham and Stan decided we should go on the terraces. He tried to disguise himself, but of course he was instantly spotted by the fans. He was one of the most famous faces in the country. Another time we went to Liverpool and Stan insisted I drive the car right up to the gate so that he could be seen getting out of the Rolls-Royce. He could be a showman when he wanted to be."

Without doubt, the highlight of Cullis's four and a half years with the club was the 1967-68 season when they finished fourth in the second division, just missing out on promotion, and reached the semi-finals of the FA Cup, where they lost to West Bromwich Albion.

In the League, Birmingham climbed to the top of the table on

Boxing Day thanks to a 4-1 home victory against Bristol City. Just as at Molineux, Cullis demanded attacking football and that brought goals galore and plaudits for being the most entertaining side in the country. The charge for promotion faltered, though, during the run-in, due to a variety of factors. Trevor Hockey broke an ankle and missed the last nine matches, from which only ten points were mustered. A change from a positive 4-2-4 formation to more cautious 4-4-2 tactics were criticised. Perhaps even more significant was the distraction of the FA Cup run, where the side reached the semi-finals. Eventually, they finished six points adrift of going up to the top flight.

Halifax and Orient were beaten in the Cup before a fifth round clash against Arsenal. Cullis's team drew 1-1 away and then won the replay 2-1 at St Andrew's thanks to a scissor kick from Barry Bridges. In the quarter-final they surpassed that achievement with a 1-0 home triumph against Chelsea, who had been finalists the previous season. The semi-final was against West Brom, who boasted fine players like striker Jeff Astle in their line-up. A 60,000 crowd at Villa Park saw Birmingham dominate the play but fail to convert their chances, although Fred Pickering hit a post. When Tony Brown shot for the Albion and hit the woodwork the ball bounced into the net. The luck was with West Brom, who went on to win the FA Cup at Wembley in the Final.

Daily Mail reporter Mervyn Thomas wrote: "Morally, Birmingham won that semi-final. I could have wept for Cullis and Coombs, the chairman. Cullis was gracious in defeat, praising Albion for taking their chances."

Cullis was criticised for playing two defenders in attack that afternoon and paying the price for excessive caution. Veteran Birmingham player Malcolm Beard said: "You have to have luck and we were out of it that day. I disagree with those people who condemned the management for playing two defenders in attack. All the chances that came our way fell to our established strikers. Colin Green and Malcolm Page played the roles they had been allocated very well. I noticed that no-one criticised our tactics after we had beaten Arsenal and Chelsea." Skipper Ron Wylie added: "Our success in the quarter-final against Chelsea was a personal triumph for The Boss. We players were told exactly what to expect and precisely what to do. We knew we could beat them if we did what we were told."

For the big matches the attention of the Iron Manager was total. This was his milieu, and he relished the business of trying to outwit opposition managers like Dave Sexton and Bill Nicholson. He had a measure of reward thanks to a new idea in football – the manager of the month award. It was started in early 1968 and the first winner in February was Don Revie at Leeds. The second announcement in March 1968 nominated Stan Cullis. Back in the 1950s he and Matt Busby would have won almost every month between them. The citation read: "Cullis was one of the outstanding managers of the post-war era with Wolves, and it is gratifying to be able to reward his comeback in this way."

It was the only tangible recognition he received as one of the greatest managers in the history of English football.

That season was proof that Cullis could still fashion a football team for a club and its fans to be proud of. But it wasn't the same as winning, and he knew that better than anyone. David Exall recalled: "Even though it was a fine achievement to take Birmingham to the FA Cup semi-final, the mood of the time was that it always seemed to end in disappointment for Stan. He would get upset and withdrawn for days afterwards. He took it all very seriously.

"The Birmingham experience was not a happy one. I stayed friendly with him for a long time afterwards even though I left in the late sixties to join Everton. Very rarely would Stan want to speak about his days at Birmingham City. Wolves was his club. He had been sacked unjustly at Molineux, and I believe he never got over that. I did once hear him come very close to swearing in public. He was talking about John Ireland – and it showed how bitter he was. I don't think Birmingham was important to him. Wolves was life.

"We used to say at Birmingham that once Stan had started talking we should have a sweepstake about how long it would be before he would say: 'Now, when I was at The Wolves'. It didn't take long before it was in his conversation."

Cullis's final ties with Wolverhampton were cut when the

family moved from the town where he had lived for more than thirty years to Stourbridge. Later Stan and Winifred moved even further away into Worcestershire, eventually settling in the picturesque serenity of the Malvern Hills.

The perception with the benefit of hindsight that his heart wasn't totally in the Birmingham City job is understandable. Cullis had surely learned from his sacking at Molineux that to give up your life for a football club would not mean repayment with endless loyalty. Nevertheless, his years at St Andrew's should not be regarded as failure. It has been rare in Birmingham's history for the club to reach the semi-finals of cup competitions and in the 1968-69 season they again performed well in the League to finish seventh in the Second Division and, scoring prodigiously again, played in front of average home crowds of 26,000, with 40,527 watching the visit of Villa and over 39,000 when Derby came.

Footballers of quality were also enticed to the club by the Cullis aura. One was centre-forward Fred Pickering, from Everton, who had won three England caps just before the 1966 World Cup, and another was Jimmy Greenhoff, signed from Leeds for £70,000. Then there was Barry Bridges, who was capped four times by Sir Alf Ramsey in that same period, and who arrived from Chelsea, a club managed at the time by the ebullient Tommy Docherty.

"I remember sitting with Stan while he was doing that deal," said David Exall. "It was quite interesting being at one end of the phone. He had me on an extension line because he wanted whatever was said to be vouched for, so that I could verify the conversations. He started bartering over Bridges when he was talking to Tommy Docherty. The Doc was a wily character, but Stan got what he wanted at the price he wanted. He was no fool in that kind of thing, he knew exactly what he was up to.

"Stan also used to have battles with reporters who came up from London, particularly over what he felt were intrusive transfer stories. He didn't like those at all. His main adversary was a chap called Peter Batt, and he had a warning system set up so that if the gateman saw Peter he would tell the secretary who would tell Stan, who would then disappear upstairs and leave me to deal with him."

What proved to be the final season of the career of the Iron Manager was in 1969-70. His team could not consolidate on two years of consistent League form and slumped to eighteenth position, narrowly avoiding relegation to the third division. A comment by Cullis a couple of years earlier about the strains and stresses of football management revealed how the job was beginning to wear him down. "I've lived with the tension, dear me, I have," he said. "You create that yardstick with success, and every time you win, that heightens the tension for you again."

In the spring of 1970, with England off to defend the World Cup in Mexico, Cullis departed St Andrew's. As he did so, ironically, another General Election was being called. Elements among the younger directors at Birmingham had been growing sceptical of the Cullis regime, and Stan himself had become less and less enamoured of the changing ways of football, including the emergence of the hooligan phenomenon. Birmingham had particular problems in that area as trains were smashed up and fans fought with their counterparts from Aston Villa.

"What made him finish with Birmingham and management was the new world of agents and money," said his son Andrew. "He felt the players and their advisers were far too greedy. I don't think he could handle that because he was more an army style of manager. The thought that players were always asking for more money and yet leading a lifestyle that wasn't the greatest – he found that very hard to take. I think it was a big factor in calling it a day. I don't think he had any offers of management after that. Perhaps there was a national team or two from the Middle East. But I don't think anything would have tempted him back in after that."

David Exall believes it may also have been a case of jumping before he was pushed. He explained: "I dropped Stan a note to say how sorry I was to see that his time had finished at Birmingham. He wrote a very nice letter back saying that he felt he had been treated unjustly by people who he had regarded as friends. Mr Coombs senior and Stan were always friends, but by that time his son was running the show a bit more. I believe that in a sense he regretted later that he had gone to Birmingham City. In his heart it should have stopped with the Wolves. He needed to work but he didn't really want to work."

"What I do know is that Stan was an absolutely cracking bloke – even if in some ways he was a little naive, because I remember him saying to me once that he had only just realised that cider was alcoholic."

Chapter Eleven

Full Circle

"....Stan Cullis was one of the great football managers of any age..." – JOHN GILES

S TAN CULLIS may have retired from football in 1970, but his passion for the game burned as a fiercely as ever. The primary outlet for his thoughts and ideas was a remarkable stream of letters to contemporary figures in soccer, many of them written and received out of the blue. If Stan saw an incident that provoked an observation, he penned a note of advice or comfort to a manager. Others went to players, or to journalists for whom Cullis had a point to make.

It was almost as if the letter-writing was a way of dissipating the tension that remained forever in his body watching a game of football. Cullis, in contrast, rarely if ever wrote to his own children who were away at boarding school receiving the best education money could buy – a luxury he had been denied as a boy.

So many football people received the Cullis wisdom, solicited or not, that a few examples will have to suffice in illustration. Ron Atkinson, once a Cullis Cub in the 1950s at Molineux, had by the 1980s become a successor to Matt Busby at Manchester United, bringing the FA Cup back to Old Trafford.

Atkinson said: "Many years later when I was a manager Stan would always stop for a chat if we were met at a match. He was still 'Mr Cullis' to me even then. He was a compulsive letter writer and I remember receiving a note from him in the post when I was manager at Manchester United. Stan had noticed that Kevin Moran was always getting cut eyes through heading incidents. He wrote to me saying that Moran should be taught to leap properly and use his arms to protect himself. That had always been Stan's trademark as a player, his arms and elbows jutting out.

"I made a point of talking to people like Stan and Billy Nicholson. You could learn so much from them, even if they weren't as high profile as they should have been after going out of the game. I recall that Stan used to have a training routine when you always had to play the ball when you received it, get it with one foot and pass it with the other. I used to think it was a fitness thing and it wasn't until later on when I went in to management and did some coaching myself that it dawned on me, yeah, that's a great little training exercise to improve your skills. We had to do the old-fashioned thing of playing the ball against the wall every morning too."

Another man to receive advice in the post was the former Leeds and Republic of Ireland midfield ace John Giles, who had become the successful manager of West Bromwich Albion after his playing days ended. He said: "When I fell out with the board of directors at West Brom in 1976 I remember Stan writing me a letter. I was objecting to the system there, and it was all very public. His letter was very nice, the gist of it being that I should remember that the family always came first and not to be upset about what was happening. It seemed to me that showed he had some regrets about his own life. The old great football managers put everything into their clubs and their family lives could suffer for it. He was telling me not to let that happen. However many trophies you win as a football manager, eventually you get stuffed. I met him a few times after that and he was such a contrast to the legend of the hard-man manager. What I do know is that Stan Cullis was one of the great football managers of any age."

A classic example of Cullis's empathy with younger modern managers was his response to the career of Graham Taylor, who guided small-town Watford to the very top of English football on the back of long-ball percentage play in the 1980s. Taylor and his club received an immense amount of flak for the playing style, even though there were also incredibly skilful players like John Barnes in the side. It was very similar to the analysis of Wolverhampton Wanderers' football in the 1950s, criticism which Cullis had deliberately manipulated to cement the spirit at Molineux.

Stan could not help but admire the work of Taylor, another intelligent man who had thought long and hard about his footballing tactics and who was unafraid to use ideas that others scorned. Taylor explained: "When I was at Watford and being heavily criticised for the so-called long-ball tactics of the team, Stan wrote a wonderful letter to me telling me not to worry and to stick to the ideas I believed in. That was very heartening at the time. There had been a fuss about his Wolves team in the 1950s, so he knew what I was going through. He wrote to me again when I was being attacked as England manager too. Those are the kind of things you really appreciate when times are difficult. Stan was very supportive.

"A few years later I became manager of the Wolves and the first thing I did when I arrived at Molineux was to read his book *All For The Wolves*. It was about the team and the way they played and trained rather than about him. What struck me was how far ahead of his time he had been, and how so many of the predictions he made about the future of football had come true. It was quite incredible. My greatest regret as a manager is that I wasn't successful in lifting Wolves back into the top division of English football."

The foresight of Cullis's ideas about the game in his book, written in 1960, are indeed remarkable. They contained both concerns about fundamental problems in English football as well as radical ideas for improving the game. It is worth exploring these to understand just how a brilliant a mind Stan Cullis had for the sport he loved.

Looking into his crystal ball he had four major worries. The first was a blind refusal to cut the number of teams in the top English domestic division in line with continental nations. "It is the immediate duty of our clubs to reduce the size of their competition so our players compete on level terms," wrote Cullis. "Perhaps we cannot cut down to twelve teams. But at least let's make it sixteen or eighteen without affecting seriously the economic structure of clubs." By the start of the 2000-01 season the Premier League still had twenty teams.

Cullis thought the consequence of too much football was a danger of burn-out, of sheer physical exhaustion. "The whole future of football in Britain depends on our ability to face the challenge from abroad, and we cannot hope to do it successfully while we work our players beyond the bounds of reasonable endurance," he explained, perhaps with Wolves' recent 9-2 aggregate loss to Barcelona in the 1959-60 European Cup in mind. The fear of player burn-out still dominates modern discussion of football in Britain.

His third worry was that skill levels were seriously below the levels of European counterparts, and he passionately argued for a two-month mid-winter break and more summer football in good weather. FIFA's proposition of a worldwide winter break to start in the year 2002 has been strongly resisted by the English authorities. England's miserable displays in the Euro 2000 tournament, where other nations were noticeably more skilful, did not seem to matter.

The fourth concern was how to deal with television coverage of football. Cullis was a radical, saying back in 1960: "I believe it can bring many new customers through the turnstiles. Although I am in a minority I am sure we would be wise to have more games screened live. Television offers an opportunity not seen in all of soccer's history, a whole new source of revenue, a vast sum which must make a considerable impact on the game. There is a danger of football indigestion, but football must be a friend of TV to flourish."

Wolves had helped to pioneer the early live TV coverage of matches against Honved, for example, and no-one can now doubt the truth of Cullis's view, made against the prevailing wisdom of his day. Other prophesies he made also came true; an extension and widening of the European Cup to allow more than one team from the major countries to take part, the creation of a world club tournament, the creation of a "Premier League" in England, the development of soccer academies at the leading cubs, the modernisation of grounds so that "watching a football match becomes a pleasure rather than a task not lightly undertaken by the old", the building of a new national stadium owned by football itself.

Why did English football not make use of this brilliant mind after Cullis retired? It is a good question to which, there seems to me, no good answer.

Instead of staying in the game he invested in Warners, a photographic business in Wolverhampton. Stan would try to help both in running the shop and in dealing with negotiations. Andrew Cullis reckoned his father was a fish deeply out of water there, saying: "He had technical problems, one of which was that he couldn't take a good picture to save his life." But the name of Stan Cullis gave the firm a kudos that was hard to improve in the town – and he worked typically hard behind the scenes. He knew no other way.

The closest Cullis came to an official role in soccer after 1970 was as a member of the panel which chose the young player of the month. Stan was the Midlands representative, and it gave him a cast-iron excuse to go to matches every Saturday and watch a new generation in action.

He was driven to games by Dr Neil Phillips, who became a close friend as well as Cullis's own GP. Phillips had previously worked as the medical man at Middlesbrough football club and knew the game well. He told a revealing tale about the ways of English football and its lack of regard for men like Stan Cullis.

"I always remember a story Stan mentioned to me about a fellow called Charles Hughes," said Phillips. "Hughes worked at the FA for years and years in various coaching positions and eventually became one of the leading men at the FA. Stan went to an Army dinner in Aldershot one night, and they had also invited Hughes, who hadn't got a clue who Stan was at all. Stan told me he was totally horrified that this chap high up in the FA didn't know him."

Former England and Blackpool full-back Jimmy Armfield, who later managed Leeds to the 1975 European Cup Final, was a fellow member of the young player award panel for a while. He has his own opinion of why Cullis was allowed to drift away from the game despite his immense contribution to English football; he believes it has much to do with the last remnants of the class system at Lancaster Gate, where working class heroes like Cullis were viewed with discomfort.

"I would put Stan in the highest group of managers," said Armfield. "He was one of people who plotted the route to change for football, he was one of the people who broke the mould, who got involved with the players. Before that players just played and were second-class citizens. In those days it was the establishment and the rest of us. That's what it was like. People don't realise that at all these days."

Cullis was never an establishment figure, and yet his interests were so very conservative and cultivated; opera, religion, military history, cricket.

The gap between the myth and the reality of Stan Cullis's character was never bridged by many in the world of football. Armfield had a glimpse when they were together on the young player panel, adding: "We had some interesting talks, about the church as well as football because I was interested in church music. It was very different to how he was as a manager. Then he would storm up and down the touchline. He would get so worked up, and shout and scream. He was also so patriotic. I never knew anyone more proud of their country."

That had been evident in his desire to serve in the war and in his passion to lead Wolves to victory against foreign opposition. In retirement it found an outlet in reading widely about the history of war and the English army. "Stan had a tremendous library on military history," said his friend Neil Phillips. "He read avidly everything he could find on the histories of regiments and battles and campaigns they fought. He could talk for hours with such enthusiasm about his time in the army. I am sure his disciplinarian style as a manager came from that time in his life.

"Stan would also talk in raptures about the players at Wolves, but never about the time he was sacked. He preferred, in later years, to remember the good times, and there were enough of those. When I was at Middlesbrough I was the club medical officer, so I'd been down in the dug-out area and if we were playing Wolves you invariably heard Stan in a rage at some point. But away from football he was so charming and such delightful company.

"I would liken his intensity to that of Bill Shankly – and it wasn't just about the result of particular matches. Stan was so dedicated to the job and was concerned with every facet of the game. I remember when he was manager of the Wolves that one of his players had quite a nasty injury at Middlesbrough. They had brought in nylon studs at the time and there was a concrete tunnel at Ayresome Park through which players ran out on to the pitch. Stan was convinced that a loose piece of nylon stud had gone up the player's leg almost like a surgical knife up. It was an enormously long and thin laceration. I remember Stan writing to me after the match to ask for my support in having nylon studs banned. That was typical of how involved he was in the game.

"He was so helpful in retirement as well. There was a time I was trying to organise a golf day to raise money for the local community health service in Worcestershire where we lived. I mentioned this to Stan and a week or two later he gave me a long list of names of footballers whom I should contact. So many of the old players turned up, like Peter Broadbent, Bill Shorthouse, Bobby Hope and Ronnie Allen. We raised £5,000 and it was all because of Stan."

While helping to raise money for good causes, the money for Stan Cullis himself slowly began to run out. He had been paid a good wage at Molineux and later at Birmingham, but it was nothing like the small fortunes that modern players and managers earn. There were no lucrative endorsements, no new life as a TV pundit. Cullis had not amassed extra money, either, by under-the-counter 'bung' payments that some managers resorted to in an effort to cash in on their years of fame.

In the early 1990s I remember Cullis walking out of Villa Park unnoticed by thousands of fans milling about outside the ground who simply had no idea that this gentle, frail old chap was one of the greatest figures in the history of English football. Such relative anonymity did not boost his bank balance. When a football collector was looking for memorabilia, long before the recent boom in value of objects like England caps, Cullis sold most of the souvenirs of his soccer career for the sum of £100. Daughter Susan said: "I remember a man turning up on the doorstep and leaving with all my father's England caps and so on. Of course £100 was a lot more money back then, but now I think that was very sad. Goodness knows where they have ended up."

By 1991 there was a very real danger that Cullis would have to sell his house in the Malvern Hills to make ends meet. It would have been heartbreaking for his wife Winifred, and yet his friends knew that Stan would never accept charity on a matter of principle. To help him would require a little ingenuity – and it came from Doug Ellis, chairman of Aston Villa, a ground Cullis often visited at the time on a Saturday afternoon.

Ellis contacted the new Wolves chairman Sir Jack Hayward, whom he knew had idolised Cullis both as a player and a manager of the club and the pair talked about what could be done for the Iron Manager. Sir Jack had personally financed an elegant rebuilding of Molineux into a stadium fit for the 21st century – a dream that Cullis had been promoting when he was a manager. Back in the 1950s Wolves had engaged architects to design an ultra-modern new 70,000 stadium on the lines of the great Bernabeu stadium of Real Madrid. It featured on BBC television programmes, but never moved beyond the drawing board and a toy model. Now, nearly forty years later, Sir Jack's idea was to name one of the new stands at the ground after Stan Cullis. A testimonial match could be held before the start of the 1992 season, to tie in with the opening of the stand, and the proceeds from the occasion could go to Cullis.

It was a perfect plan to which Stan and his family happily agreed. Ellis said: "I was delighted to be able to play a part in that testimonial because he and I went back a long way together right to Ellesmere Port as well as the time at Birmingham City. Stan would come to watch matches at Villa, and I learned more from him about football than anyone. He was always very keen to know, for example, about the background of a player, whether he had the right character for the club. I've had a few managers, as people know, and I always ask them about the character of a player when there is a possible transfer being discussed."

Such is the affection that Wolves fans continued to hold for Stan Cullis nearly thirty years after he was sacked that the ground was full, and the day raised more than £70,000, money which meant he and wife Winifred continued to live in the family home together until she died. Now it still helps to finance his peaceful existence in a nursing home in the Malverns.

Son Andrew said: "Doug Ellis was very good to my father. He was instrumental in getting the testimonial organised, and it proved to be a good healing of the rift. At the time he said to me, 'It's come full circle Andrew.' He was never one for showing or expressing emotion, but my father was touched then. He was very pleased about it, walking out on to the pitch before the game and receiving a wonderful ovation from the crowd. The emotion was quite extraordinary."

The stand chosen to be named after Cullis was the old North Bank, home of the noisiest section of the crowd, the huge, imposing terrace on which, in the words of Geoffrey Green, "the Molineux crowd had surged, tossed and roared like a hurricane at sea, and called for the kill," in the famous 1954 match against Honved. The choice seemed entirely appropriate because Cullis had always been a man of the people.

In his old age Cullis suddenly acquired a new fan club. Son Andrew explained: "He was always amazed when we took him to Molineux late in life how many people wanted his autograph, especially the youngsters. One of them wanted him to sign a Wolves shirt with a big felt pen, and it was a girl. This was quite incredible to him. After that testimonial day he went back a few times to be involved in the Wolves Former Players' Association, of which he became president. He was very pleased that he was back in the fold again at Molineux after all the bitterness that had surrounded his sacking. I'd love to be able to tell my dad before his time is up that Wolves have reached the Premier League, reached the top of football again."

In the last few years Stan Cullis has been unable to attend football matches any more. Nor can he write the stream of letters to people in the game. His memory has declined with his health so that he cannot remember the great moments of his life in soccer.

This happened to many other famous managers, including Bob Paisley of Liverpool and his old schoolboy friend from Ellesmere Port, Joe Mercer. Both of them were afflicted by Alzheimer's Disease. Doctors believe that Cullis has a different condition, a form of dementia that has similar unhappy consequences.

Stan's children are certain that his condition is a direct result of his days as a professional footballer playing with the tough leather balls of his time. The serious concussions which Cullis suffered throughout his career caused his premature retirement. He suffered mini-strokes as a manager. It seems more than mere coincidence that other football men from the same era were struck by health problems in later life.

It is an issue from which officialdom has shielded its gaze. Cullis's daughter Susan wrote to the Football Association a couple of years ago to ask them to hold an inquiry into the matter. She has never received a response.

Stan Cullis, it seems to me, has never received the proper respect from the game of football that he deserved after a lifetime of intensely passionate service as player and manager. He is the oldest living England football captain, a sportsman who lived and played by the highest principles, a patriot who gave tremendous service in the war, a centre-half who reacted with dignity when the dream of winning League and FA Cup winners' medals so narrowly eluded him, a football manager who was a colossus of the game, a man who inspired the creation of the European Cup.

Men like Bill Slater are surely not wrong in believing that Cullis should have been rewarded with suitable accolades by the country for which he felt such patriotism and loyalty. In the modern day royal honours are awarded for far less than Cullis achieved.

It is too late now to correct that shameful wrong. Stan Cullis passed away peacefully in February 2001, the news announced on the day England played a friendly against Spain at the Villa Park ground he knew so well. A minute's silence was observed before the start, with his grandsons James and Ben among the respectful crowd paying tribute to one of the giants of English football – to the Iron Manager.

Bibliography

ALL FOR THE WOLVES. Stan Cullis. Rupert Hart Davis 1960.

THE WOLVES – THE FIRST EIGHTY YEARS. Percy M. Young. Soccer Book Club. 1959.

ONE HUNDRED CAPS AND ALL THAT. Billy Wright. Soccer Book Club. 1962.

JOE MERCER – FOOTBALL WITH A SMILE. Gary James. ACL and Polar Publishing. 1993.

MASTERS OF SOCCER. Maurice Edelston and Terence Delaney. The Naldrett Press. 1960.

FOOTBALL AMBASSADOR. Eddie Hapgood. Sporting Handbooks. 1948.

FOOTBALL IS MY BUSINESS. Tommy Lawton. Sporting Handbooks. 1946.

STANLEY MATTHEWS – THE AUTHORISED BIOGRAPHY. David Miller. Pavilion. 1989.

FOOTBALL IS MY GAME. Stanley Mortensen. Sampson Low. 1949.

FOOTBALL FROM THE GOALMOUTH. Frank Swift. Sporting Handbooks. 1948.

WOLVERHAMPTON WANDERERS GREATS. David Instone. Sportsprint. 1990.

TALKING WITH WOLVES. Compiled by Steve Gordos. Breedon Books. 1998.

THE FOOTBALL LEAGUE 1888-1988. Bryon Butler. Macdonald Queen Anne Press. 1987.

THE EUROPEAN CUP 1955-1980. John Motson and John Rowlinson. Queen Anne Press. 1980.

THE FOOTBALLER'S COMPANION. Edited by Brian Glanville. Eyre and Spottiswoode. 1962.

SOCCER CHOICE. Bryon Butler and Ron Greenwood. Pelham Books. 1979.

PEOPLE IN SPORT. Brian Glanville. The Sportsman's Book Club. 1968.

Bibliography

GREAT MOMENTS IN SPORT: SOCCER. Geoffrey Green. The Sportsman's Book Club. 1973.

THE OFFICIAL HISTORY OF THE FA CUP. Geoffrey Green. Heinemann. 1960.

SOCCER REVOLUTION. Willy Meisl. Phoenix Sports Books. 1955.

EUROPEAN CUP 1955-1980. Anton Rippon. Mirror Books. 1980.

CAPTAIN OF HUNGARY. Ferenc Puskas. Cassell. 1955.

THE FOOTBALL MAN. Arthur Hopcraft. Sportsman's Book Club. 1968.

40 YEARS IN FOOTBALL. Ivan Sharpe. Anchor Press. 1952.

SOCCER REBEL. Jimmy Guthrie. Pentagon. 1976.

STANLEY MATTHEWS – THE WAY IT WAS. Headline. 2000.

ENGLAND – THE FOOTBALL FACTS. Nick Gibbs. Facer Books. 1988.

Index

Index